LOST TEENS, LOST FAITH

*A Guide to Engaging the Souls
of the Next Generation*

DEREK BIRD

WESTBOW
P R E S S®
A DIVISION OF THOMAS NELSON
& ZONDERVAN

Scripture quotations are from The Holy Bible, English Standard Version® (ESV®), copyright © 2001 by Crossway, a publishing ministry of Good News Publishers. Used by permission. All rights reserved.

Scripture taken from the King James Version of the Bible.

All Scripture quotations in this publications are from The Message. Copyright © by Eugene H. Peterson 1993, 1994, 1995, 1996, 2000, 2001, 2002. Used by permission of NavPress Publishing Group.

Scripture taken from the Holy Bible, NEW INTERNATIONAL VERSION®. Copyright © 1973, 1978, 1984, 2011 by Biblica, Inc. All rights reserved worldwide. Used by permission. NEW INTERNATIONAL VERSION® and NIV® are registered trademarks of Biblica, Inc. Use of either trademark for the offering of goods or services requires the prior written consent of Biblica US, Inc.

WestBow Press books may be ordered through booksellers or by contacting:

WestBow Press
A Division of Thomas Nelson & Zondervan
1663 Liberty Drive
Bloomington, IN 47403
www.westbowpress.com
1 (866) 928-1240

Because of the dynamic nature of the Internet, any web addresses or links contained in this book may have changed since publication and may no longer be valid. The views expressed in this work are solely those of the author and do not necessarily reflect the views of the publisher, and the publisher hereby disclaims any responsibility for them.

Any people depicted in stock imagery provided by Thinkstock are models, and such images are being used for illustrative purposes only. Certain stock imagery © Thinkstock.

ISBN: 978-1-5127-2600-8 (sc)
ISBN: 978-1-5127-2601-5 (hc)
ISBN: 978-1-5127-2599-5 (e)

Library of Congress Control Number: 2016900066

Print information available on the last page.

WestBow Press rev. date: 01/14/2016

To my wife, Jenn, for her love and support
and for pushing me to live God's will.

To my boys, Carson and Jaden, for the sacrifice they had to
make on my account. May God bless you richly for this.

To my parents, Gary and Sandy, for showing unconditional
love to your son and for raising me to have hope and faith.

To my brothers, Jason and Chris, for fearlessly using your
skills to make a difference and for being an example to me.

To all my students, but especially the 2014 Grad
Class (please forgive me for taking a sabbatical
during your most important year).

CONTENTS

PREFACE

A year or so after graduating, Patrick walked back into my classroom and sighed as he placed his latte on one desk and situated himself on top of another desk directly across from mine. He did it in such a way he initially made me think he had never really left. He slumped and sighed again. "Mr. Bird, it's raining outside, and I was bored so I thought I'd drop by and see how you were doing," he commented.

After ten minutes of covering superficial topics, Patrick went on to tell me exactly how life was, and it was not good. His girlfriend had just broken up with him, and she was off to university. As a result, he'd quit his job in order to spend more time with her so he could win her back, but he completely failed because she had broken up with him because she wanted a guy who had more direction and more drive. It was a vicious circle. Patrick sat in front of me and sipped his latte, completely broken, completely confused, and completely wondering what his purpose was in life.

As he continued to speak about his present situation, it became clear the reason he was not moving forward with his life right now had nothing to do with ambition. He wanted to do something, and not just anything; he wanted to do something great for God. It's just that Patrick could not figure out what that might be. He'd spent lots of time in prayer, but for whatever reason, God would not provide him with clear direction. He had two desires but could not choose between them. So he sat trusting that God would tell him whether he should become a youth pastor or a teacher. The year went by, and God still had not clearly revealed to him the way he should go. Steeped in directional paralysis, he felt like God had betrayed him.

I couldn't help but wonder if, as one of his teachers, I'd failed him in some way. All the hype in high school and the "You can do whatever you want to accomplish" had essentially kicked him in the face. I felt a weight with the realization I was part of a Christian community that had not provided him with key answers to critical questions. What's sad is that Patrick had to deal with the same questions I had dealt with at his age, and he was no farther ahead than the teenage version of myself.

What I went on to talk to Patrick about on this particular day took me nearly twenty-five years to fully figure out in my own life. His demeanor changed when I said, "What finally helped me overcome this immense confusion was when I realized that what I chose to do as far as career was secondary to the way I performed the daily tasks required by that career. From a human standpoint, we can never know for certain what God wants us to do for a career. He will guide you, and you can only live trusting you will honor God with the skill set he's gifted you with, as long as your deepest desire is to honor God. In other words, go become a youth pastor or a teacher, all the while offering your life as a living sacrifice to your Creator." This made sense to him and relieved a deep tension. He walked away from our conversation ready to make a decision and then move forward in his choice.

The words that follow are for my students like Patrick and Cameron, for Jade and Brandon, and for Brian and Brielle. The words are from your teacher, but more importantly, they are from a fellow traveler who walks life's road just a little ahead of you and has taken the time to chart out some maps that will make navigation for those who follow just a little less confusing. These words are for my generation and for generations who follow and are motivated primarily by that which prompted King David to write, "So even to old age and gray hairs, O God, do not forsake me, until I proclaim your might to another generation, your power to all those to come" (Psalm 71:18 ESV). You are the next generation to take up his words and dispense them to your children and to the hurting and lost.

And in order for the Christian faith to remain healthy, those of us who go before must always be willing to realign with truth, then be willing to teach the generations who follow; otherwise, we could see the Christian faith falter in our culture in a way we've never seen it falter before.

A few years ago, the school board I worked under stumbled across a concerning statistic. One of the members read a Barna Group statistic stating that over 70 percent of children from Christian families will not return to the church after they graduate from high school. The individual then presented her findings to the rest of the board, and they set a course of action based on the reasoning provided for the enormous attrition. The primary reason tagged to Christian children leaving the faith in droves had to do with intellectual skepticism.

My purpose here is not to discuss the intricacies of the findings, because really a digression like this would predominate the conversation and only exemplify the real issue but never delve into it. Generally speaking, Christian culture is preconditioned to engage the mind and spend countless hours exploring the compounding questions of "What if?" and "How many?" How many return to their faith like a prodigal son or daughter would? Or like one Calvinist parent asked me when I retold this story during a speaking engagement, "What if these children are not really saved?"

But what if for a moment we stripped away our need to explain every detail and to justify the Christian faith by questioning the authenticity of a young person's salvation commitment? What if, conversely, as a parent we assumed a large number of the students polled were telling the truth—that they left the faith because of intellectual skepticism? A response would be quite different and maybe even lead to a solution rather than a justification.

The school board took it at face value and created a plan based on what would seem entirely logical. If teens, once they've graduated from high school, leave the faith because they arrive at a point where their faith does not make sense to them on an intellectual level, then they need to learn to think through their faith in a way that they can safely navigate through the questions they have or the ones that are posed to them. Acting on this logic, the school board decided to go in an apologetics direction. They planned a conference for the high school kids to expose them to some of the greatest Christian minds in the region. Highly regarded university professors came and spoke, and the kids listened attentively.

After the apologetics conference, I asked a number of students about the benefits of the arguments presented and if they felt better prepared to think through and defend their faith. A great portion of their answers surprised me. A number of them responded in a very similar fashion. To summarize, most of the students stated that they found the speakers very engaging, but that they'd heard most of the arguments before. Interesting. A great portion of Christian students leave the faith because of intellectual skepticism, but they have already heard and have some understanding about how to argue and rationalize their faith.

What's the solution then? What can we do, as parents raising the next generation, to ensure our children continue to desire Christ? First, I think the most important step we could take is to respond rather than react. A *reaction* comes from an isolated part of our brain where the result can only ever be fight or flight. And I'm not suggesting for a moment that we discontinue engaging a teenager's mind. That would be fleeing the apologetics scene.

A *response* to this issue requires an individual to use a portion of his or her brain that is a collector and dispenser of wisdom.

And wisdom says as a faith culture we have learned too much to disregard the teaching of rationalization and understanding of the faith. This must continue. However, I would suggest, generally as a faith culture, the Christianity of recent generations has elevated the mind above other essential components. So when Christ says to love the Lord God with all your heart, soul, and mind and to love our neighbors as ourselves, he invites his followers to love God and fellow humanity with the entirety of their beings.

In other words, because of the faith culture in which our generation grew up, we potentially present our children with a gospel that elevates the mind. Think for a moment about the community of believers your parents raised you in. If it's anything like me, you would have learned to define your faith by the denomination your were not. You would have learned early the key components of your denomination and how your statement of faith differentiated you from other Christians from, say, an Alliance church or a Baptist church. Eventually you would have also come to an understanding that learning about the faith, discussing the faith, and debating the faith promoted the deepest connection to God. We've become possibly the most cerebral Christians to ever walk the earth—filled with deep knowledge yet lacking a deep connection.

Following this line of thinking, it's little wonder that our children fall away because of intellectual skepticism. Unintentionally and erroneously, we've taught them that to know God with their minds is the highest order. So they graduate from high school and head off to trade school or to university and are challenged by peers and professors; they know all the answers, but they lack connectivity because the Christian faith is not designed to be an entirely intellectual activity. And because we've taught them to intellectually defend their faith and we've indirectly taught them they can fully defend their faith from a logical high ground, when they realize they can't, their entire faith world crumbles. Generally speaking, our parenting generation has done an adequate job of teaching our children to defend their faith but a very poor job of living their faith. Only by combining the two do we instruct our kids to follow Christ's greatest commandment and do we lead our children to experience an authentic faith.

We have to continue to raise our children in an atmosphere where they learn to love God with their minds, because Christ commands this. But we also have to reengage the forgotten components—the heart and soul—to complete the whole. A person can never love God with the mind alone. God did not design the faith relationship this way. He created humanity in his image, intending a dynamic interrelation of these key elements.

This book takes root from the passion to create a shift in Christian thinking. Throughout the following pages, I address fundamental faith concepts extremely pertinent to a teenager's stage of life. These ideas are discussed in a way to reengage the entirety of the individual. For when Christ redeems us, his redemption encompasses heart, soul, mind, and strength.

PART 1

A FUSION OF PURPOSE

CHAPTER 1

Discovering the Generational Foundation

A few weeks ago, I read an article in *MacLean's* magazine entitled "Get Ready for Generation Z." Author Anne Kingston defined the generation as "those born after 1995 and who are now 18 and under."[1] Though the article touted some of the challenges Gen Z faces, it mainly focused on all they had already accomplished and praised them for being ambitious and innovative. This next generation wants to change the world, and they know how to use the technology to do just that. They are environmentally sensitive, racially aware, and "less likely to subscribe to traditional gender roles."[2] Not only this, but they are more morally aware as well. They don't drink, smoke, or fight as much as previous generations and are less likely to involve themselves in sexually risky activities.[3]

The article went on to talk about specific examples of kids who are already making a difference from child inventors to magazine editors to chefs.

I felt somewhat enlightened after reading the article. Normally there is so much doom and gloom discussion surrounding future generations. In the Christian circles, we can be especially bad for this. I have friends who never wanted kids because of the current state of the world. And then there are the old-timers who think that the world is doomed to hell because my generation can't seem to figure out how to raise children properly. Though it was good for me to hear who's in the on-deck circle as far as children, I couldn't help thinking about the ones who are not the high achievers. I've taught high school for enough years now to understand an axiom: every generation will produce motivated individuals and every generation will produce unmotivated individuals. Each generation is not immune to challenges. So though there is much optimism about the up-and-comers, we can never forget a key fact. Some people will fit into generational norms, and some will not. Furthermore, some will start out on an extremely positive trajectory only to fade out into their early thirties. And the opposite will be true. Some will be late bloomers. And some seeds may not germinate at all. So though there is much reason for optimism, one can never be lulled by the positive, nor should we be deflated by the negative.

Amidst all the reading I did about generations, and even with the positive tone of Kingston's article, I can't help but think of my old friend's daughter who recently ended her short seventeen-year life. She was part of Generation Z. Interestingly enough, she was not the antithesis of the child inventors or magazine editors in that she was extremely intelligent, and her parents provided her with all the opportunities she needed in order to succeed. She went to good schools and had access to excessive amounts of technology and information, yet somehow in all this, despair overwhelmed her. And she's not the only one. This past year, I've spoken in different places all across Canada, and wherever I go, people are looking for answers as to why, in this time of privilege, we continue to lose students to suicide at the rate at which we do. Even as I researched this chapter, my mother called me and told me about her friend whose young son just ended his life. Is there some subverted disconnect? Generation Z has all the potential in the world. They possess access to everything, but they are also in real danger of not truly connecting to anything.

The week after I read the article praising Gen Z, I stumbled across an article in *Time* magazine that also talked about Gen Z, but in a completely different way. The article was not actually about generational gaps or generational analysis; it was simply about the short life of one particular Gen Z kid. The article by Jack Dickey, titled "The Antisocial Network," explored the tragic suicide of fourteen-year-old Matthew Homyk. The Ohio teen ended his life after months of online bullying. The ninth-grade student used Ask.fm, a web site with millions of users worldwide.[4] It's a place where mainly teens go to post messages and interact, but they can do so anonymously. Because of the anonymity of the site, people are able to post messages relatively free of consequence. Here, teens allegedly posted cruel messages to Matthew that ultimately played a factor in his death.[5] Sound familiar? The article states, "Since 2012, press reports have suggested that Ask.fm was a factor in at least 16 adolescent suicides in the US and Europe."[6]

The two articles side-by-side present a more complete picture of the new generation arriving on stage. The two pictures together essentially say Gen Z is loaded with potential, and we may even get to see an end to cancer and heart disease as the brains from this generation develop and become educated and inspired. We may get to see solutions to global warming and energy shortages. We may see a generation who finds alternatives to war. Limitless possibilities exist. However, part of the portrait includes individuals who still carry with them emotional scars too great for them to bear. They may feel betrayed by relationship and by a greater awareness of all that exists out there, coupled with the fact they may not be able to have access to all that they desire. A deep disconnect may result from the gap between all the information they have access to and all they desire to accomplish. The valley between the two is as deep and wide as a vast canyon. As parents, our greatest failure may be that we are not teaching our children how to negotiate the canyon of perceived possibility. Our children get to see what's on the other side, but they have to learn to climb steep, treacherous terrain in order to arrive at the other side. And it's our responsibility as parents and educators to give them the tools they need in order to hike along the unforgiving path between reality and their dreams. Of all that we teach our children, our teens, there may be nothing more important than educating them in the area of purpose. A clear understanding of purpose allows them to survive the deep tension between the way life is and what they desire it to be.

Generally speaking, our parenting generation needs help in this area though. All we've ever learned, through culture as a whole and within the wall of the church, is that purpose exists in a single dimension. We've striven so hard to figure out what that one thing is that we've forgotten the search for the one reason actually blinds us to a greater reality. The church takes the statement near the end of Ecclesiastes, that humans exist to "serve God and obey his commandments," and makes this the beginning and the end of the discussion. In context, however, the speaker in the book lives a full life and arrives at this place. Is there a way we can teach our kids about life's purpose without beginning with the solution? For certain, we are here to worship God and to glorify him and obey his commandments, but how do we do that? How do we get there? Why do we start with the end when teaching our teens, who are infant adults? For many kids, this is a disservice, because they now have very little understanding how interconnected life actually is. They do not see that many areas of life require sacrifice, and when we do this for Christ, it transforms into an act of worship. Whatever we work at, when we do it for Christ, we perform the task as an act of worship. When we raise our kids to follow the moral precepts of the Scriptures, this becomes an act of worship. When we work as a baker or a professional athlete, a pastor or a pediatrician, a janitor or a junior salesperson, we do it as an act of worship. But because we've started with an end, we have possibly, unknowingly, created problems in a few areas. One is a detrimental hierarchy of occupations: a senior pastor, a youth pastor, and a missionary. And then all the other less spiritual occupations fall somewhere below. An integrated understanding of purpose encourages a young individual to begin their career search with the skill set God provided them with as opposed to a false inflation of occupation.

A faulty view of purpose leads children down a confusing path, and this path dead-ends at insecurity. When we teach our children to look at purpose as a single dimension, our kids will be more susceptible to defining themselves by how others view them. The problem with this, especially through the teen years, is that they are surrounded by insecure people who generally hide their own insecurities by preying on the insecurities of others. As parents, we can provide them with a new understanding of purpose, and in doing so, we hand them the antidote to the venomous cycle.

The other day, I was reading Luke 19 and became fascinated by the brief narrative of Christ's encounter with Zacchaeus, which ties together the connection between insecurities and purpose. What strikes me the most about this man is what most people know most about him: he was short. In some translations, he is short, and in others, he is small in stature, which is really the same as saying he wasn't tall, which is really the same as saying the man was short. So whatever way you look at his encounter, he's noteworthy because of his atypical stature.

And just in case a person might miss the passage discussing his size, most Christian youngsters also sing a song about the vertically challenged man. I remember singing the Zacchaeus song countless times in my years at Sunday school, and with over 355,000 hits on YouTube, the song seems to have survived to the present time. The lyrics begin with "Zacchaeus was a wee little man and a wee little man was he."[7] So really by the end of the first two lines, the writer has established and reconfirmed Zacchaeus's diminutive stature. Not just once but twice. And to reinforce his size, he uses the adverb *wee* to emphasize the adjective *little*, which then describes the noun *man*. So how small was he? According to the song, the tax collector grew to an abnormally wee little size and then stopped growing. It might be safe to assume Zacchaeus is biblical antithesis of Goliath.

In our culture, we also have wee little men who end up compensating for their stature by body building or inflating their personality, which in turn is the originator of the phrase "short-man syndrome." For this reason, I'd also assume Zacchaeus had the Hebrew equivalent of short-man syndrome. My guess, and it's only a guess, is that he got bugged and ridiculed because of his height when he was growing up. The boys may have picked on him, and the girls may have rejected him because he did not meet a culturally acceptable average. So even if he was naturally relational, he found out quickly in life that others may not accept him in a way he desired to be accepted. He may have ended up going through a time of depression as a result of the deep hurt. But instead of allowing it to destroy him, he went in the opposite direction. He found another cog on the wheel—one that not only provided him with a good income but one in which he could excel because of all the derision and ridicule he received as a teenager. He'd grown calloused to the opinions of others because he'd heard too many jokes at his expense.

Who would have thought that would end up being a life skill he needed in his line of work? But it was all worth it now, because he was wealthy and in a far better place than those who had tortured him earlier on in life. Come to think of it, he even had power over those people. Oh, how life turned in his favor.

He worked through the ranks and ended up becoming the chief tax collector—top of the ladder careerwise. He'd accomplished all he'd ever set out to accomplish and much more. I wonder how long he was here before he began to wonder if there was more to life. There must be more. One day he heard about a rabbi coming to town. He may have even heard this teacher called Jesus presented teachings that were far different from the usual.

He'd heard the usual and found that they never helped him with his greatest challenge—his desire to be accepted in the face of constant rejection. So Zacchaeus took a break from work one day and ambled down the road in hopes he'd be able to listen to this new teacher. But when he arrived at the place where Jesus was to pass by, the crowds had already gathered. And with him being, well, you know, he could not see through the crowds, yet something deep within him caused him to fight the urge to turn around and head back to his safe house. He looked around and saw a tree rising above the large group of onlookers. His small stature allowed for him to make it past the large group without having to make eye contact. He, out of anyone in his town, knew the difference between a stare of derision and eye contact signifying friendly human contact. He longed for one, yet he was all too familiar with the other.

When he got to the tree, he grabbed the first low branch and pulled himself up. And as he climbed higher, more and more people began to notice him. Again, the jeering started. With each branch, the jeering got louder until he reached an elevation where no matter who he came to see, it just wasn't worth it. So he peered over the unaccepting crowd and, without a word, began to go inward. He began to repress all hurt his callouses had protected him from. He thought, *What was I doing climbing a tree anyway? I just set myself up.* About halfway into his retreat, the crowd grew quiet, and above the newly established silence, he heard his name. Zacchaeus did not turn, for he knew if he acknowledged the voice that all he'd hear was another "short" joke. So he placed his foot on the next lower branch and heard his name again, followed by an urgent command. "Zacchaeus, come down immediately. I must stay at your house today" (Luke 19:5 NIV). Jesus? It was seemingly impossible, but with a phrase, Christ redeemed the tax collector. Zacchaeus came down quickly and welcomed Jesus into his home.

While coming down from the tree and walking away from the crown with his new guest, the muttering started up again, but this time, Zacchaeus hears a different side. The crowd implicates him by referring to him as a sinner, but more surprisingly, they begin to deride the great teacher, the new rabbi they came out to see. They huff and hiss and say, "He's gone to be the guest of a 'sinner'" (Luke 19:7 NIV).

Zacchaeus takes note of something he's never understood before. This person who the crowd came to see, who they were excited about listening to, who had miracle-performing abilities, the group talked down to him. For the first time in his life, he realized even the most ground-shaking individual ever to come to his town was also ridiculed. Maybe the ridicule never did originate from his own shortcoming but from the shortcomings in others. Without a word, except for his name and self-invite, Jesus had just revolutionized his life. The hurt others caused him all these years was the result of others projecting their own hurt onto him. Their hurtful words were the result of their own deficiency and not his. His deficiency was simply a target and a way for others to avoid their own (possibly less obvious) deficiencies.

As they walked toward his house, this epiphany caused the tax collector to turn to Christ and enthusiastically proclaim, "Look, Lord! Here and now I give half of my possessions to the poor, and if I have cheated anybody out of anything, I will pay back four times the amount" (Luke 19:8 NIV). With his newfound relationship and understanding, Zacchaeus reaches out to reestablish what he desired so much. He rediscovers purpose beyond selfish movement in a single direction. He feels restored. He feels reborn. For the first time in his life, he forgets about how short he is. Then Christ explains his purpose. "The Son of Man came to seek and save what was lost" (Luke 19:10 NIV).

The Conclusion of the Matter

So really, regardless of what kind of potential a generation has been labeled with, there is an element of need that exists. Earth is beautiful and full of resources, and its inhabitants are full of creativity and ingenuity and drive and desire, but the flip side existed from near the beginning of time and will continue to exist until the end of time. A cruelness and coldness also exist, which seems to infiltrate even our hearts and souls. And as a result, along our eighty-year journey, we can become discouraged and bitter and depressed. Essentially we can lose our sense of purpose, causing us to lose passion. This can happen to anyone, regardless of wealth, power, or social standing. Again then, I say, without exception to the overindulgent baby boomers, the confused Gen X, the narcissistic and self-absorbed Gen Y, or the potential-filled and coddled Gen Z, we all have the ability to lose hope and a sense of purpose along life's trail. Really then, what we all have in common is that we end up in one of Zacchaeus's stages. Either we are downtrodden because of hurt we carry around, we are compensating for the hurt, we are goal driven for selfish purposes, we are searching for a better reality, or we have come down from the tree and are walking with Christ.

So how do we provide our kids with an understanding of purpose congruent with their stage of life? One that provides them with a greater chance of walking with Christ through this life?

CHAPTER 2

Lives of Purpose

So many interesting but unknown words exist in the English language. One that's always fascinated me is *borborigymous*, which is onomatopoeic in nature and means the internal sound gas makes as it rolls through the intestines. It's more than the gurgling sounds and is more the uncomfortably loud noise that strikes at the most inopportune times. Another little known word, but just as unessential to an individual's word bank, is *callipygous*. Should you ever desire to use the word, it is an adjective referring to one who has a firm or tight buttocks. Or what about *jumentous*, which means to smell of horse urine, as in "The portly young farm boy could not extricate the jumentous odor from his cowboy boots after the horrendous barnyard accident."

You'd think, with the nearly one million words available, I could find one of those little-known words to discuss at this point, and I probably could. But I'm going to discuss one we've all thought about before, probably a lot, and one we would have no trouble defining. But it's one philosophers, theologians, and scientists have argued about for centuries. The word possesses a concept central to humanity, and individuals as far back as Adam and Eve probably wondered about the idea. I think it might be safe to assume no matter place or time, a person's mind drifts onto the concept. So take a moment and think about the word *purpose*, and I'll get back to it in 1,481 words.

Because I teach high school, I can get singularly focused on achievement, especially around provincial exam time. One of my greatest desires is that my students do well on the exam, so they feel like they've achieved something in high school. I want them to do well, because if they do, then they feel like all their hard work paid off. Accomplishment. I reward this as a teacher. A student who accomplishes much means they learn much. One of my students—I'll call him Hansen—figured this out as a youngster. When he came into my classroom for the first time in grade 8, he came dressed for success, complete with tie and dress pants. His intelligence preceded him. Other teachers let me know I was in for a good year because Hansen was in my class. And he proved to be a teacher's dream. Well behaved, intelligent, and driven—what more could a teacher want? With Hansen in class, discussions elevated to unimaginable levels. Finally, a student who understood Shakespeare, who picked up the subtleties of each play we covered, who wrote engaging essays, who consistently displayed upper-level vocabulary, who dissected poems at a level university professors would be proud of.

As years passed, his intelligence grew exponentially, and by grade 12, I could not wait until he took the provincial exam. When the time came, he did just as I expected. Top marks. He truly was the epitome of what our culture considers a successful student. If only more Hansens existed, we could have hope in the future. But he did seem to have one flaw that followed him through the years: he could not relate to his classmates. Because he succeeded in an institution built for kids like him, he looked down on others. His intellectual arrogance proved to be a problem in junior high, but by senior high, when the majority of students began to realize the importance of working hard to achieve a mark, he became more popular, especially during group assignments. Everyone wanted

Hansen for a partner, because he enabled the students around him to attain better marks.

Another student, who like Hansen always seemed to be engaged in class, comes to mind. Tamera was somewhat studious but made her presence known in another way. She was the rule keeper in my class, and because it was a Christian school, she made it her job not just to police the hallways and classes for rule infractions, but she also kept an eye open for the moral infractions as well. She could only be described as a budding legalist. I am sure she came by her legalism honestly, and at her age, she had very little self-awareness or situational awareness when it came to how her air of superiority affected not only herself but also those around her. Tamera took a stand against almost everything, so she alienated herself from the majority of her classmates. She had a few good friends who seemed to follow her and who she dragged along with her into major battles. Not only that, but she memorized the Scriptures with fury and knew them better than all of her classmates, so she could beat them down when it came to debate. A few students could stand there blow for blow with her, but her tenacity in putting a halt to the pollution of the school and the Holy Word of God (memorized in KJV) always proved to win out in the end.

One day I entered her line of fire when I told my English 12 class I'd be showing the movie *Dead Poet's Society* the following day. Though the movie is rated PG, after class, she informed me she had already seen it and had some serious concerns about one of the scenes. I told her she did not have to worry because I skip one of the scenes. She said, "Oh of course you'd skip the cave portion of the movie. The boys are smoking and looking at a bad magazine." I replied, "Right, thank you for reminding me of that. I'll be sure to fast-forward that part as well." I'd forgotten all about that event from the movie and had the suicide scene as the primary concern for my English 12s. Then Tamera responded by saying, "How could you forget about the cave scene, and why would you worry about the suicide scene? That scene is fine." An interesting statement. So in Tamera's mind, it's fine for Christians to watch a suicide scene but not okay for us to watch characters smoking or looking at inappropriate material. I'm not condoning either in a Christian classroom setting, but I'm concerned about Tamera's thought process. When morality becomes a primary focus, we fool ourselves into believing we are more spiritual and more righteous than those around us and that we've cornered the market on right and wrong. When we do this, an imbalance exists in our lives and we tend to forget that Christ's message of grace and redemption provides a realistic human error element to his message of morality. When an individual becomes singularly focused on morality, he or she can only end up living a life of duplicity.

That said, my classroom is riddled with students who could learn a lot from Hansen's study habits and Tamera's moral attention. Unfortunately, but for a clear reason, these types of students tend to alienate themselves from others. The classmates who normally do not want to associate with the studious types or the rule-keeper types are the same "students" who only earn the title because they show up to school and occupy a desk. When they can get away with it, they'll use the top of their desk as a pillow and try to catch up on the sleep they were deprived of the night before because they gamed into the wee hours of the morning.

Joshua was this guy. He had shoddy attendance at best, and when he did show up, he was usually late. He'd saunter into class completely unprepared, because he learned if he came without his books, he'd have to leave class to get them. He'd be able to delay the inevitable for just a little longer. Because Joshua was sleep deprived, he rarely engaged in class discussion, and all his assignments were late if he ended up handing them in at all. When he had to write a creative essay, the only way I could get him to write one was if I encouraged him to write it about his

15

only interest: gaming. He'd write at length, and when he turned in the essay, I'd feel like, as a teacher, I'd accomplished something. Joshua was a bright kid, but he'd learned somewhere along the way there was something more important than school. I had many conversations with him and his parents, stating he might not pass the semester if he did not hand in his assignments. He had the potential to be a strong B student, but he cared little about grades. Not surprisingly, he gravitated toward others who could match his gaming enthusiasm.

Lots of reasons exist for avoiding schoolwork, not just gaming. Another common one is relationships. Aniston worked hard in her younger years, but then she discovered boys in junior high. She couldn't put a thought on paper without it pertaining to relationships, and when she had to write about a topic, which had nothing to do with her favorite subject, she'd draw more hearts on her page than words. In class, she couldn't concentrate because of the young man she crushed on that particular week. She'd figured out the importance of proximity in relation to the young man who unknowingly captured her affection. Stage one of her conquest involved placing herself in desk where she could stare at him without him knowing. After a few days in that desk, she'd disrupt the usual flow of the class by taking a desk within a four-seat radius, so she could be placed in a group with him when I required group work. After this stage, she'd make it her goal to sit directly in front of him, so he could not help but notice the way she dressed or see her hair on his desk as she'd throw back her head in false contemplation. In this placement, she could also turn around and ask him for help when she struggled understanding a concept, which coincidently was quite often because she paid little attention to the instruction in class, for her mind could not be burdened with the unimportant while filled with strategies for landing the young man of her dreams. Sometimes, her cunning worked, but when it didn't, she'd find another victim and start the process all over again.

Looking back, all these students have one thing in common. They all unknowingly perceive *purpose* as a fragmented concept, and why wouldn't they? Our culture commonly endeavors to reduce purpose to one clear path, one clear concept. We want to know the essence of life. If we could just have an unwavering understanding of what we're here to do, then we could weigh all else against that and decide whether or not it's worth all the pain and all the struggles. I've tried multiple times in my life, and I've even taught my students what I thought it was. I remember telling them at one point that we are put on this planet for the purpose of love: to love God and to love one another. Then a year or two later, I realized I could reduce that idea even a step farther, so I taught them God placed us here for the purpose of choice: so we may learn to choose him in the face of challenges and all that pulls us away from choosing him. So was it love, or was it choice? Maybe the essence is a combination of the two. Maybe God placed us here to choose to love him. That sounds reasonable. There's only one problem with this. It's also a fragmented approach to purpose. Though we want to reduce it to one concept, this desire may not allow one to experience life to its fullest. We end up producing a generation of children who are like Aniston, like Joshua, like Tamera, and like Hansen. They go hard in one direction and then at some point, when the direction fails them, when they face broken hearts, when they realize that they're forty years old living in their parents' basement still conquering levels, when they realize that achieving much in and of itself has nothing but emptiness in store for them at the end of the treacherous mountain path, then they head out to rediscover a new form of purpose. Why were we created if not to achieve, if not to enter a relationship, if not to enjoy creation? The truth, like so much in life, is not found in singularity but in balance.

It's so essential not to skip steps when teaching our children about what God created us to do with the time he's given us. Though it's true our purpose is to love God and follow his commandments, by not developing in our kids an understanding of what this ultimate purpose pertains to, we fail to produce a generation who understands the importance of what to apply this concept to. And what we apply this to actually provides a balanced understanding of life. Concerning purpose, our reason for why we exist in this universe is fully skipped when we tell our teens, "No matter what you do, love God and follow his commandments." Though this is true, to state it this way takes importance away from why God created us. To love God and keep his commandments is the gel, the glue, which runs through the purpose for our existence and holds it together like shores contain the ocean. There is much to be explored and much to make our teens aware of within the water. It's time to move beyond a fragmented understanding of purpose and develop an understanding of why certain desires run through humanity's veins.

CHAPTER 3

Back to the Beginning: Why Are We Here?

One of my favorite parts of the teaching year is a trip I plan for my outdoor club where we travel to the north end of Vancouver Island in the first weekend in June and spend a few nights camping on a rugged and untamed Pacific beach. The nearly two-hour drive on logging roads keeps the crowds away, but once on the beach, with tents set up, watching the evening sun set over the endless expanse of the blue ocean makes the bumpy road and all the planning more than worth it.

The planning can be a hassle, to say the least. Trying to prepare a group of fifteen students for a hike-in campout into a remote location is a bit of a headache, especially if any of the students owns an overprotective parent. They call constantly with questions about toilet paper, and granola bars, and cougar, bear, and wolf warnings. But I endured all of this, so I can take my group to an area of unparalleled beauty.

Last year I'd suffered through the pain of planning and was getting ready to simply enjoy the trip when tragedy struck. An old friend of mine, who I hadn't seen in years, had a seventeen-year-old daughter who ended her life. I received word the celebration of life would take place at the same time as the campout. I'm embarrassed to say I was torn. I tried to convince myself I needed to be on this campout for the kids' sake, especially for the ones graduating. They needed me to be there; this was their last year. But in my heart, I knew where I needed to be on that particular weekend. I needed to be supporting my friend Todd and his wife, who were experiencing what no parent should ever have to endure. I gave the reigns of the campout to another teacher and then made plans to attend the funeral.

There's no good time for a funeral. Generally, in our society, we are always too busy, even to attend a tragic event of this magnitude. But once we're there, they have a way of adding a certain perspective to life. The campout, for example, once I was at the funeral listening to the sorrow-filled speeches, seemed so insignificant. I could not fathom even for a second why I questioned attending. Funerals—death—they have a way of doing this. I listened as the young lady's classmates and friends got up and spoke. The speeches were raw, as tears salted each spoken word. Most of them wanted to know why. Why would she do this? She was so beautiful and she had lots of friends. She had her entire life ahead of her. Though many of her friends spoke of their different memories together, they all at some point grappled with *why*. They searched for an answer to an unanswerable question.

When my friend got up to speak, he did not even have to say a word as he gripped the pulpit for support, and those present shared in his brokenness. Those who knew him understood what he was about to say was more than just out of character for him; they knew it went against what seemed to be major foundation on which he'd built his life. Todd worked hard through high school and university. He achieved good grades as he studied to become a mechanical engineer. Once complete, he moved into the workforce and, again through intelligence and work ethic, progressed in his field of expertise until he moved into a position where he managed other employees and earned an extremely good salary. Admittedly, he did not accumulate wealth for the purpose of keeping up with the Jones, but he did so for the noble purpose of providing a good life for his family. Intelligence and hard work, by all appearances, seemed to be primary motivators in his life.

Yet his daughter's untimely death seemed to make him question the philosophical platform on which he built his life. In his brokenness, he stated, "There must be something more. I don't know what it is, but there must be something more to life." Even with his self-sufficiency, his intelligence, and his wealth, the passing of his daughter forced him to look beyond the tools he'd used to construct his life to that moment.

Funerals have the potential to expose our souls to a point where raw emotion bubbles forth like a simmering pot of soup. As mourners sit in the pews, we weep, and we grapple with the finality of death, the moment compels those present to wonder about life's purpose and whether or not we are accomplishing that purpose. Death asks us to take stock of what we've done to that point in life and makes us realize there must be something greater— some greater reason for existence than working, acquiring wealth, buying expensive cars, and then moving on to some unknown, everlasting sleep. In the words of my old friend, "There must be something more."

Why Are We Here?

Ashamedly, I don't go back to Genesis very often, and the last few times I did, a guest creationist lecturer directed me to go back. I followed him through as he logically built points about how each day was only one day and could not represent millions of years. As fascinated as the church has been on the debate, the first few chapters contain information equally relevant to that of origin: they also discuss humanity's reason for existence. And what it says about purpose reveals, generally speaking, that our culture may have a very misguided view.

21

It's no coincidence that, when I sat observing the funeral procession, I myself reflected on existence and meaning. According to the first few chapters of Genesis, death is related to the fall of humanity, which is discussed in close proximity to the origin and purpose of humanity. God's curse on the earth ends with a reminder of our finality: that all of us at some point will return to the dust from whence he created us (Genesis 3:19 NIV). Though many do all they can to prolong life, hoping one day someone will truly discover the fountain of youth, in pertaining to a beginning and an end here on earth, our days are numbered, so what can we glean from the musings about our origins regarding why we were placed here? Maybe if we developed an understanding in this area, we could make the most of our time here. Maybe we could experience a deeper purpose so we don't get so sidetracked performing tasks for the primary purpose of purchasing a four-wheeled piece of finely tuned German engineering that goes like schnell. Though very cool, there must be more.

Tend to the Garden

Todd (my friend who lost his daughter) and Hansen (my bright student who I discussed earlier) have a portion of truth regarding purpose according to the first few books of Genesis. God placed us on this planet to work, to accomplish, to create, to problem solve. When God created us, he gave us instructions almost as clear as Lego directions: subdue the earth, and rule over the fish and the birds and every living creature (Genesis 1:28 NIV). God reduced the task for Adam and Eve, maybe to make it more manageable, so he created a garden and then placed them in the east quadrant of Eden for the purpose of working the ground and taking care of it (Genesis 2:15 NIV). It's no wonder, however many millennia later, in our culture we've created institutions that prepare our children for the workforce.

We praise children like Hansen, who've learned at a very young age we exist to accomplish much. The more a child accomplishes, the more he's praised for accomplishing. Thus, the cycle begins. At first, we give children stickers when they satisfactorily complete a task. After they outgrow stickers, we allow them to achieve letter grades. We take a letter from our alphabet, and we make it stand for a symbol of achievement. Then we hold it out and say, "If you earn an A, you are doing well, and if you earn a C, you are performing at a satisfactory level." With all its flaws, for the most part, the system works, though by grade 12 some students become fairly tired of the achievement symbols. This same concept transfers to university, and then once in the work force, instead of creating a letter to symbolize achievement, we use paper, then we assign it a value. The more paper we earn with numbers on it, the more we can buy. A person can buy bigger and better items, which we also refer to as symbols in a way. Our houses and cars and boats and toys can be status symbols. The more we earn and own, the more people respect us because they desire what we have—the lifestyle and the wealth. And the more we own, the more self-sufficient we become.

I don't mean to make this life cycle sound hollow, because really, work, if it is a purpose for our existence, can't be meaningless; otherwise, our existence is meaningless. So why is it this cycle potentially ends in a person wondering if there is more to life than working and buying and amassing? If this is what God created us to do, then should we not feel satisfaction in creating, in grappling with ideas, in building, in performing? The answer is yes, because an omniscient God would never have created us for such a shallow existence. This purpose can become shallow if it is treated as a singular purpose rather than part of a collection of purposes for why we exist. The problem with viewing life entirely through the "accomplishment" lens is an individual begins to view all other reasons for our existence through this lens as well. When understood in light of the other reasons for our existence, work and creating become a way of connecting to the very core of our being.

Through our work, we create, we entertain, and we feel a sense of accomplishment because we connect to a skill set. Humans possess the tools needed in order to tend to the garden, and what we don't possess we have the ability to create. So when we learn and when we accomplish, we experience a sense of connectedness. This connectedness exists because people use their skills to fulfill an original purpose. Why then can an individual experience a sense of accomplishment from a task and then from the completion of the same task weeks or months or years later they can feel an emptiness? That's an interesting question leading one toward exploring intention and design. Hansen will get there, to the same place as Todd, at some point. It might take a family crisis or the monotony of the daily grind. It might take a few career changes or buying all he's ever dreamed of buying and still feeling like there's got to be more, in order for him to get there. But in my mind, anyone who is singularly focused on accomplishing will arrive one day at a point where they state, "There must be more." At that point, a person has a few choices. The most common outcome though is disregarding work as a purpose for existence and refocusing their exploration pertaining to a life of meaning.

This is an extremely difficult place to come to, because it means far more than an individual simply working less. The lifestyle driven by one's belief in accomplishing as a purpose affects the entire way they see life and interact with those around them. If people live to accomplish, and they find purpose in this, then they must also view other key aspects of life through this grid. Relationships, for example, become about this. Relationships serve a purpose, and that is to help you conquer, overcome, improve your status, make you look good, or elevate your social standing. With this outlook on purpose, relationships become a way to help an individual fulfill a purpose.

We go through life focused on what we think is most important: a job, relationships to make us better at our jobs, and relationships to move us forward at our jobs. Then something makes us look at life from another angle and we see all we've been missing. So we head in that direction for a while and again look from another perspective, seeing all we've been missing. We then begin to ask, "What is the right perspective? What is our actual purpose?" If it's not work and accomplishing and creating, then what is it? It is this, but this is not all it is.

To Rest and Enjoy

While standing in a grocery lineup, I ran into parents of a former student. I asked them how Charlie was doing, expecting the usual formality of "He's doing just fine." Instead, they said, "He's not doing so well." And then they launched into a conversation lasting beyond paying for groceries; it spilled out into the parking lot. They explained a feeling of helplessness. Charlie, now in his early twenties, rarely left the house. He couldn't hold a job because he stayed up late into the night and slept most of the day. They didn't want to kick him out but felt like they had no alternative. Was that all they could do? Practice tough love, a short-term relational sacrifice for a long-term benefit? As they spoke, I thought back to Charlie as a high school student. He had trouble handing in assignments and was quite often sleepy and unengaged in class. He cared little about any of the literature we read and felt it a waste of time to delve into any themes presented by the writers. When he wrote essays, he wrote about his deepest passion. All he ever wanted to do was game. Now a few years out of high school, he was living his dream. According to his parents, he gamed well over forty hours a week. Impressive. That's a full-time job.

I actually did not have a lot of advice for his parents. I just listened as they kept coming back to the concept of tough love. They knew they needed to do something harsh like destroy the gaming system or just kick him out, but they feared they would lose him if they did either of those. At forty hours a week, and neglecting other essential aspects of life, Charlie's addiction to gaming was costing him his life. His parents' harsh love concept might be the only way they could save him from himself.

There's a reason Charlie's love for gaming turned into addiction. As a balance to work, God also created humans to relax and enjoy his creation. He desires for us to appreciate the smell of rain on a hot summer day, to enjoy the panorama from the top of a mountain, to cherish the refreshing feeling of diving into a cool lake during a mid-August heat wave, and to be attracted to beauty, whether it is in nature, music, poetry, or painting. When God created, he "made all kinds of trees grow out of the ground—trees that were pleasing to the eye and good for food" (Genesis 2:9 NIV). Included amongst these trees were the Tree of Life and the Tree of Knowledge. The name *Eden* means "delight," and the description of the garden matches its name. After the speaker discusses two trees associated with morality, he takes what I've always considered a sidetrack. He does not explain right away that Adam and Eve are not to eat from the Tree of Knowledge; instead, he detours. He carries on describing the setting, Eden's beauty. The garden possessed a river that irrigated its flora. From the garden, the river separates into four, which is backward really. Normally a river gains in capacity as it is joined by smaller streams in its drainage. But in Eden, the source of the river springs forth from the garden and then fans out into four separate rivers, providing life-sustaining and refreshing waters beyond the garden's parameters.

According to humanity's origins, our desire for rest, enjoyment, and entertainment has deep roots. We've come a long way since the garden. We can still admire creation while hiking and camping in remote and pristine locations, and some still do, but North Americans seem find other more popular diversion tactics, and judging on the amount of hours we spend we spend doing it, we are also addicted to diversion. Our desire to be engaged in entertainment starts young. Some studies indicate that by the time a child is eight years old, they are spending an average of eight hours a day using different forms of multimedia, and teenagers are using upward of eleven hours a day. How is this possible? Some of the hours measured are part of media-multitasking. A teen might be on their iPhone with a friend, while at the same time watching a movie and playing music in the background. I realize a portion of media usage has nothing to do with entertainment, and may have more to do with communicating with friends. If it's social networking (teens spend an average of three hours a day at according to Ipsos Open Think Exchange), the line between relationship building (or destruction in some cases) and entertainment may be too blurry to make a distinction between them. Humans possess a natural desire for diversion and entertainment, and because of technology, we have never had easier access to solutions for this need.

According to a study done in 2013 at the University of Southern California Marshal School of Business, the average American will consume 15.5 hours of media per day by 2015. A person does not have to go far though to find organizations calling for a balance in this area. The American Academy of Pediatrics recently recommended children should not consume more than two hours of screen time per day and they should not have TV or Internet access in their bedrooms.

It's not just time spent but dollars as well. An article on Billboard.com stated that entertainment industry will top two trillion dollars worldwide by 2016 and the United States is to account for almost 30 percent of this staggering statistic. A person can see how the large numbers would add up. According to the Statista.com, 111.5 million viewers watched the 2014 Super Bowl and an average thirty-second advertising spot cost four million dollars. Though the NFL is an entertainment blockbuster, the gaming industry holds its own when it comes to capturing our free time interest. In the States, 58 percent of the population games and over twenty billion was spent in the gaming industry in 2012,[8] and global citizens spent 93 billion dollars in the gaming industry in 2013.[9]

Like in Eden, people still enjoy the scenery as well, just to a lesser extent. More than forty million people in the United States go camping each year, and spend about 1.8 billion dollars on camping equipment annually.[10] Mixed into that number in some way, about forty-eight million people in the United States fished in 2013.[11]

God created us to enjoy the garden that we tend to, but our teens can easily become unbalanced in this area, like Charlie did. When we pursue relaxation and enjoyment alone, either in forms of human created entertainment or naturally created entertainment, when we forget we've been created for multiple purposes, this can generate a skewed version of reality. Generally speaking, we must work in order to survive, and we must take some time to appreciate our surroundings in order to truly feel alive. The two, tending to the garden and taking the time to appreciate the garden, are both necessary aspects of life. Though, in this case, balance unfortunately does not mean a scale with equal amounts on either side. Balance here means we learn to work and create with the majority of time we have, and we learn to enjoy that which we've created and what God has created with a much smaller portion of the time we have.

Moral Choice

God also created us as moral beings. We have choices to make in life—wise and good choices, poor and sinful choices, challenging and indeterminate choices. Some decisions we make have little to do with morality, take choosing an ice-cream flavor (unless you're overindulging) or standing in the cereal aisle completely overwhelmed by all the different breakfasts-in-a-box companies offer. But many of our choices tie in some way to morality. We can choose to date someone, but once we've engaged in this type of relationship, there are plenty of moral dilemmas that bubble to the surface. We can start a business, and before long the entrepreneur faces moral dilemmas regarding areas of honesty and integrity. An individual can sit down to dinner and choose to overeat, or sit down with their iPad and choose to be part of the approximately 25 percent of all Internet searches leading to a pornographic site. Why so many moral decisions? Along with our desire to work, to accomplish, to create, God also created us to make moral decisions.

By Genesis 2, God already has a very interesting discussion with Adam. While simultaneously discussing the beauty of the garden, he draws Adam's attention to two very important trees: the tree of life and the tree of the knowledge of good and evil. Right after God places man in the garden to "work it and take care of it," (Genesis 2:15 NIV) he goes on to command, "You are free to eat from any tree in the garden; but you must not eat from the tree of the knowledge of good and evil, for when you eat of it you will surely die" (Genesis 2:16–17 NIV) God allows them to choose eternal life in a garden of unsurpassed beauty, with unhindered relationship with him … or … death. Sometimes, I wonder if God fully explained the outcome to Adam and Eve, would they have chosen the same path. Or if Adam would have simply asked a few questions, I wonder if all the trouble and turmoil would have been avoided. A simple question like "God. What do you mean by death?" To which God could have at least created a quick word picture of what he meant. He could have said, "I mean death, you know, absolute human agony stemming from war and famine and disease. Toss in a little emotional turmoil like hatred, bitterness, anger, greed and insecurity, and you start to get the picture. But just in case you don't. Imagine never feeling at peace with yourself or your surroundings, and always feeling like you're standing on a ledge between wondering if you need me or don't need me. And imagine all the decisions you have to make could lead to a lifetime of turmoil and confusion, but instead of turning to me you turn to what I've created and you find medicinal plants which you light on fire so you can ingest the smoke hoping you'll be able to cover up pain, confusion, or find a level of comfort in the midst of the mess you've made of your life—you know Adam, death."

I suspect, even with this limited picture, Adam would have done all he could to avoid the tree. The truth is, prefallen humanity possessed no frame of reference, no understanding of what existed on the other side of the decision to disobey God's command, and had God communicated this to him in some way, the decision would have not been much of one to make. Remain in perfect relationship with God and the land he's created or the alternative. So even prefall humanity had moral choice to make, for this is one of the reasons we were created.

This purpose for our existence, within our culture, I would venture to guess, is not seen as a purpose. Though we live the results of our decisions, and the choices we make in our youth carry a life-long impact, we've reduced moral decisions and choices to nothing more than choosing a flavor of ice cream. Personal morals are now more of a preference. Which, please don't get me wrong, I don't think morals should ever be legislated unless they have to do with a serious infringement on another person's well being. Telling a person how to live becomes far more detrimental to a culture than freedom of moral choice affecting an individual's well being. That said, if an individual is central to their universe, then morality can be relative. However, the moment individuals believe they are part of something greater than themselves, morality can no longer be relative. In our quest to make ourselves the most important component in a world filled with components equal to ourselves, we find ourselves living out the concern God expresses after he banishes Adam and Eve from the garden for their universe-altering moral decision. They've eaten from the tree, so not only does sin enter the world but also in the same bite, the knowledge of good and evil, the understanding of right and wrong, becomes part of humanity. And every one suffers from this knowledge, because our understanding is limited by time and space. So we have knowledge good and evil exists, and now we are tasked to differentiate between the two, yet we are inhibited by human nature and an inability to see beyond the present. This is where the issue of moral relativism leads an individual in Western culture. They have to make the best decision they can with the tools they have.

Generations are taught to discover for themselves what is good and pleasing, what is right and wrong, and they are taught to do so as they navigate through waters they've never been through before. The possession of the knowledge of good and evil, then allows an individual to make decisions based on their own preferences at a fixed time period. So a teen can have sex with their girlfriend or boyfriend and this according to our culture is up to the individuals, as long as both sides consent, there is no issue. And really this is true to a point for those individuals at that particular moment. What's lost is a weighing of how this decision affects the future. What's lost is the wisdom transcending generations, and cultures, which speaks of saving this act for a spouse. Humans have knowledge, yes, but very limited understanding of the eternal implications associated with the moral choices we make. For this very reason, as I go around and speak I encounter a superficially functioning culture. To those around us, all is fine. We hold our lives together. At a deeper level, people in our culture hurt deeply because they've lived a life believing they could do as they pleased, and believing they made the right choice as long as they weren't hurting others. Many carry on in their destructive behavior even into adulthood because they can't see there is a way to live, which does not destroy the self. There is a way to live where we don't have to carry on with the shame or guilt of the poor moral choices we've made. We don't have to self-medicate in order to wake up every morning and enjoy the newness of the day.

At the center of our purpose in this area, is the knowledge we possess because we've become godlike. God states one of his deepest concerns just before he banishes humanity from the garden. He says, "The man has now become like one of us, knowing good and evil" (Genesis 3:22 NIV). Even before the fall, humanity had a moral choice to make. We could choose to obey God or not. But with our understanding of the existence of the "good/evil" dichotomy, we now place ourselves in a realm where we possess some of the same understanding, but are not the same being. Therefore, we've become godlike in our knowledge. The cultural push toward a moral relativity is directly connected to an individual's godlikeness. This is why, "There is a way that appears to be right, but in the end it leads to death" (Proverbs 14:12 NIV). The "like" portion means we see time not as God but as fallible humans; therefore, we see moral complexities, but we do not have the omniscient perspective to discern the fullness of a moral conundrum. Thus, generally speaking, our culture is morally shortsighted. We can't see the importance of treating others as we would ourselves. We don't understand the need to deny our own humanness in search of a higher calling, and in the end we become slaves to that which we assumed would liberate us. This concept, in and of itself, leads me to view morality as a central component to human purpose.

An opposite exists to the morally relative, and that is the morally superior. Though not exclusive to the church, faith circles are the most common arena to find individuals who take great pride in their elite moral status. There are those who subvert morality, yet there are those who unknowingly exult it as well. If you spend any time in church, you can't help but run into this type of person. The person who treats morality as most important is the same person who becomes the judgmental legalist.

Why then do some Christians struggle in this area? I don't think I need to discuss at length why we are susceptible to this sin. It's fairly obvious. We are humans in a fallen world, and our relationship with Christ is dynamic not static. So we constantly need to choose to serve Christ, not necessarily to be saved, but to choose him above our humanness. We walk a path that leads to relationship and self-restoration when we choose our redeemer over sin. His grace runs deeper than our sin, but self-righteousness takes hold when we accept his grace but can't extend his grace to others.

My concern is not so much with whether or not Christians fail. We do. My concern is for the times where we don't allow others to morally fail. This instance becomes an example of a singularly focused purpose. When an individual thinks they've cornered the market on moral truth, and when they think they've got it all together, they become the judge of those around them. This is an example of an individual who's contaminated moral purpose. They understand morality but they do not understand its necessary counterbalance grace.

Because moral responsibility is a central reason for why we were created, we can shun it or we can become engrossed in it. Culture generally shuns any type of central morality (outside of the individual); whereas, the Christian faith generally gravitates toward a moral standard existing independent of the individual which is predetermined by God's Holy Scriptures so as to strengthen our relationship with him and create peace over a life time. As Christians, though we believe in a higher standard, we're required to be extremely careful in imposing our standard on others. Though God requires us to live by a higher standard, it is not this higher standard that saves us. The moral standard which we uphold is done out of obedience to God, and is not done in order to redeem our souls but to allow our souls to remain unfettered by guilt and sin, which destroy our ability hear God's voice in our lives. Most assume the opposite of moral living is amoral living, which it is. But when morality becomes the singular focus of an individual, a strange regression happens.

In this case, when a Christian makes morality the central issue, they become godlike in this area, and they begin to pedestal themselves—they become self-righteous. They become the servant who is forgiven a large sum of money but then turns around and will not forgive another's debt to them. Morality then takes on a certain level of darkness and in this case its opposite is not amoral living but grace. God provides grace as the balance to morality.

This is why C. S. Lewis in *Mere Christianity* stated, "A cold, self-righteous prig who goes regularly to church may be far nearer to Hell than a prostitute." Matthew 18 supports this. In the second parable presented in the chapter, Christ places a servant in two positions: one as a person in need of a forgiven debt and the other as a person who needs to forgive someone of debt. To emphasize the main point, Christ places a far higher value on the debt the servant is unable to pay back to his master. The master orders that he and his family and all his possessions are sold in order to repay the debt. The servant falls to his knees and begs the master to take pity on him. The master does so, cancels his debt and sets him free. The forgiven man, instead of enjoying his freedom and extending freedom to others, instead of sharing in the same grace he's been granted, goes out and finds a fellow servant who owes him money and grabs him by the throat, and demands repayment. When his fellow servant is unable to do so, the forgiven man has him thrown into prison until he can repay the debt. When the master hears of this, he summons the wicked man and questions his actions. The master rhetorically states, "Shouldn't you have had mercy on your fellow servant just as I had on you?" (Matthew 18:33 NIV). An important lesson for all of us who've been redeemed by Christ's blood. The wicked servant is one who's been forgiven, but who can't extend the same mercy and grace to those who also need forgiveness. The master becomes enraged and sends him to jail to be tortured until he repays all he owes.

Those of faith who become consumed solely by moral living gradually become the unmerciful servant, forgiven themselves but unable to extend the same grace to others. Our desire must be Christ first, before morality, before righteous living. Those then become extensions of our love for Christ. If it is not, if we gradually fall into a "morals" first life, we become an individual in need of deep grace but unable to recognize our most urgent need. We become self-righteous, legalistic, isolationistic, and prideful; we pedestal ourselves in our blind quest to become godlike.

Relationships

In 1991 millions of people connected with the Bryan Adams's song "(Everything I Do) I Do It for You." An integral part of the *Robin Hood Prince of Thieves* soundtrack, the song not only spoke to many about the lengths a person would go for a relationship, the movie also provided a visual for the sacrifice discussed in the lyrics. The lyrics make a number of bold relational claims. The speaker would do everything for his lover. He'd fight for her, lie for her, walk the wire for her, yeah, he'd die for her. Wow! He'd be willing to give up everything for his love. Likewise, the singer Meat Loaf (I can't say I fully appreciate either the singer or the dish) in 1993 in his chartbusting song "I'd Do Anything for Love (but I Won't Do That)" makes gigantic claims about the lengths he's willing to go to for his romantic relationship. He sings through many assertions in the song as to what he would do including running "right into hell and back," which theologically may not be possible—though I don't think the writer of the song was concerned so much about the biblical accuracy of the lyrics—and building "an emerald city with these grains of sand," but the singer is willing to set some guidelines as to what he will and won't do for his significant other. "He won't do that" is exactly what he won't do in the name of love. For the longest time I, and apparently most listeners, had absolutely no clue what exactly "that" was, and I remained in ignorance for a full twenty-one years. Apparently Meat Loaf states four things he would not do for love, only two of which I'm comfortable describing. One, he won't forget the way she feels right now, and the other mentionable is to stop dreaming about her every night of his life: no he would not do that.

Adams's and Meat Loaf's songs both topped the charts, one for his willingness to do everything for his woman and the other for being willing to do anything for love (except for that). The point in all this is that millions of people loved these ideas. They connected to the lyrics for the same reason millions of people love the movies *Love Actually, Shakespeare in Love, The Holiday, Dan in Real Life,* and *The Proposal.* Generally speaking society is fascinated with relationships. We want in them; we want out of them. Relationships can make us feel like we're on top of the world, and they can also drop us to our knees in emotional torment. It's not just romantic relationships but also friends and family. Individuals who see relationships as the essence, the very core of why we exist, are usually the same people who are willing to give up everything for those they love, whether the sacrifice is positive or negative. So why is this?

My purpose here is not to explain that relationships are important, that might be on par with trying to convince people water and air are essential aspects of life. I think we get it. Most of us come to a point, either on our deathbed or early on in our elementary-school-years, where we naturally gravitate toward relationship, so there is an obviousness about this. What I do think needs to be discussed, what our teens can so easily miss out on, is the importance of maintaining a balance of purpose within relationship. Though I'd concede to the fact that relationship is a primary reason for our existence, they have the potential to easily deteriorate and eventually push a person toward isolation if he or she is not willing to view relationships in light of the multiple reasons for our existence.

Once again back to the beginning. God created humanity for relationship: both with him (which I'll talk about in the next chapter) and with others. Right after he creates us from the dust, he commands us to be "fruitful and multiply," (Genesis 1:28 NIV) which appears to be a more calculated purpose for our existence. However, when the creation of humanity is described in the second chapter, a new dimension is added. Multiple humans of different sexes are not merely created for procreation, but also because God recognizes that it is not good for an individual to be alone (Genesis 2:18 NIV). So prefall we needed each other. God did not create us to exist in isolation; he created relationship to dissolve our aloneness. Relationship is an essential component of humanity's purpose.

An irony exists at this intersection though. Relationships dissolve our feelings of isolation, yet relationships also have a very real potential to drive one to isolation. When relationships alone become our focus, a person will more willingly give up anything and everything in the name of friendship or romantic love, and here is where we need to be careful. Please stay with me through this, because I'm not saying a person should not be willing to give up their life for a friend or a loved one—that is a heroic and noble act. So in a way I'm saying giving one's life is actually not giving up everything in the name of relationship. What I am saying is a person who is willing to sacrifice the other purposes (morality/work/rest) for relationship, is the same person who is willing to sacrifice their life in an ignoble way. Take sacrificing our moral purpose, for example, for relationship. Generally speaking, a person who does this in the end creates self-confusion and emotional torture.

Take my friend John. He just entered a relationship recently. To do so he sacrificed a lot, almost everything in fact. John loved this lady he involved himself with, so much so he struggled completing the tasks associated with his daily job. Throughout the workday, he constantly texted her; he couldn't help it because of the love he felt for this woman. The texting and the sneaking away from the jobsite to be with her eventually cost him his job. John's boss no longer trusted him to be the person he required him to be. According to his boss, who was an acquaintance of mine, John just couldn't focus on what needed to be done; he became a liability and a safety hazard around the work area. Not only was he sneaking away from the jobsite, he was also sneaking away from his wife and two kids, who eventually found out. I guess you could say John sacrificed everything for love. Though most people struggle with accepting a moral standard, it would be safe to say, most people could come to an understanding that John stepped out of what would generally be considered morally acceptable. He crossed a line for a relationship, though he already had family who loved him and depended on him.

I realize this is an extreme example, but it provides a framework for what can happen when an individual becomes singularly focused on an unhealthy relationship. Really, we end up sacrificing ourselves. We can sacrifice in an unhealthy way. And when we do this, relationships actually end up producing the opposite of companionship. They can actually drive us to a place of isolation, where we can't trust enough to enter a relationship, so we end up retracting our borders to the place where we're the only one who can comfortably fit in. This merely serves as a reminder our sole purpose for existence cannot be human-to-human relationship alone.

Blurred Lines

I've oversimplified. It's tough to teach a concept without breaking it down into categories. In a person's mind divisions make more sense. But the ultimate truth extends beyond teaching our children that purpose exists in four categories. If a person ends with this notion, they are no better off than searching for meaning down a singular avenue. Though I've divided the four, in life the four cannot be separated; they intermingle like Aquafresh toothpaste. As a person squeezes the refreshing substance onto their brush, one can't help but be intrigued by the blue, white, and red pattern. Realistically though, each color touches the other, and as it fulfills its ultimate purpose, as it lathers in the mouth and freshens breath and cleans teeth, it ultimately becomes one. So it is with our four purposes in life. A person may focus on one and neglect others, but the times when a person draws closest to a connection, is the same time purpose experiences balance, and the only way purpose can be balanced is when an individual develops an understanding that they are not at the center of achieving purpose. A person must be willing to give up their life in order to fully experience life. This, I believe, is the essence of all tension. Do we strive to be godlike, or do we become God's children?

CHAPTER 4

Wagon Wheel Theology: From godlike to God's

To this point in my discussion of purpose, all I've done is to replace the thought that we exist for one reason with the understanding that humans actually exist for four reasons. Leaving the discussion here, without providing colligation of the four, would be neglectful on my part. My desire is to replace a linear understanding (we're born, then we search for the one reason we exist) with a model more congruent with what the Scriptures teach and with what one actually observes in the normalcy of life. A complete model reflecting an individual's purpose, must also allow for one more reality: the concept that humans are not only physical beings but also spiritual beings. I'm sure many possibilities exist but the model I'll provide you with is comprised of both the linear (to represent the physical) and circular (to represent the spiritual). A model possessing both aspects more closely reflects what the Bible tells us about the image of the God who created humanity.

When I think of what I've learned about purpose, I'm reminded of the old wagon wheels at the ghost town I worked at during my university summers. On a side street leading to the town's water tower, there was a graveyard of sorts for old equipment. Throughout the half acre filled with archaic farm equipment from lost generations, there were a number of old broken wagon wheels. The spokes originate at the hub and then support the outer portion or the felloes. After a century, it was far more common to see a broken felloes than one which remained intact.

A clear model for better understanding purpose is much like a fully restored wagon wheel, the only difference being the number of spokes. As discussed previously, the reason God placed humanity here is to tend to the garden, to engage in relationship, to make moral choices and to enjoy the garden. Each of those reasons represent a separate spoke in the wagon wheel. Aside from the spokes, wagon wheels also possess a hub (the self) and the felloes, which is the outer wheel section (the result of the redeemed self).

The Hub and the Fractured Self

The hub is somewhat of a complicated portion of the wagon-wheel analogy. For the hub represents the self and the self is often not easily understood. In relation to purpose and redemption, the Scriptures provide a clear description of the self. Humanity is created in God's image, yet because of the fall, we are tainted by sin nature. Christ's sacrifice and redeeming blood, however, allows for everyone to be restored. That said, God created us with choice, and we can choose to accept him and his plan or we can choose to reject his plan for redemption. For this reason it's important to make a distinction between the fractured self and the redeemed self. Both can be placed at the center or the hub, with completely different results regarding purpose. With the redeemed self in the hub a person chooses to deny self and instead chooses to follow Christ's lead. However, with the fractured self at the hub an individual chooses to do what is best for self in a particular time and circumstance. This, I believe is at the very essence of why our culture understands purpose as a linear concept.

Nowhere do I see a more condensed portrayal of the fractured self play out than in Shakespeare's *Macbeth*. Without belaboring a summary, at the narrative's inception, King Duncan praises Macbeth for his valor in battle and for protecting Scotland against invading forces. Macbeth is one of King Duncan's most trusted men. But because of predictions by witches, symbolizing an appeal to the darkness of human nature, Macbeth sets off in a destructive direction in order to selfishly achieve all that's owed to him in life. He becomes completely immersed in attaining that which the witches falsely promised him. In a flurry of violence, he digresses with one poor choice after another, all in an effort to satisfy the fractured self. First he kills Duncan. Then once Macbeth is chosen as the king's successor, motivated by his own insecurity, he orchestrates his dear friend Banquo's death because he saw him as a threat to the longevity of his reign. After creating terror throughout his country with his murderous spree, his countrymen turn on him and while he's held up in his castle waiting for battle, the news of his wife's death reaches him. At this point, he's living his choices. His occupation, his position in life, he's achieved the highest position of power, but he's paid dearly for the pursuit.

Because of Macbeth's linear movement up one spoke, advancement in career and position (tending to the garden), the other reasons for existence essentially become subservient to the acquisition of what he assumes to be most important. He kills friends and foes alike. As a result of his poor moral choices guilt initially affects his ability to sleep and eventually affects his sanity so that he's not able to feel normal emotion. He also sacrifices relationship in order to achieve a position of status. As a culmination of all his efforts, he states to himself one of the most tragically poignant quotes in Elizabethan literature. When he hears of his wife's death he says,

> Life's but a walking shadow, a poor player,
> That struts and frets his hour upon the stage,

And then is heard no more. It is a tale
Told by an idiot, full of sound and fury,
Signifying nothing.

In other words, after experiencing all life has to offer, after living the life of a king, Macbeth states that life amounts to nothing but hollowness. He says our existence amounts to nothing but a mediocre actor who pretends on stage and then passes away and then is completely forgotten.

Comparisons exist in our culture as well. Like Macbeth, celebrities have it all: fame, money, and power. They've experienced all that life affords. They have as many friends as they desire. They can be a voice and make a difference like very few others can. Celebrities stand at the pinnacle and most people want to be like them. But because they positioned themselves at the top, they also know what does not exist there: the reason for our existence. For this reason, it's not uncommon to hear of a movie star who is in and out of rehab, or divorced a number of times, or who takes his own life. I know this happens throughout our culture, but it seems to be especially prevalent in this group because, by all appearances, they lack nothing.

Celebrity and Shakespeare's tragic hero present an interesting truth with regards to purpose: in order to experience a life of purpose, humanity must recognize our inability to achieve, on our own volition, a life of purpose. When we place ourselves at the center in our quest to discover purpose, we will only ever end up chasing a mirage; our quest is flawed from the outset because humanity is flawed. Pursuing work alone, we can become workaholics. Pursuing enjoyment alone, we can become narcissistic pleasure addicts. Pursuing morality alone, we can become self-righteous legalists. When our origin is the flawed self, the end result is a disillusioned self.

Left to our own desires, humanity can only ever fully pursue one spoke. We can only filter our lives through work and the desire to achieve, or through relationships, or through morality, or through relaxation and enjoyment. On our own we can never accomplish a balance between each purpose and thus when we've come to the end of one path, or felt betrayed by another, we can only arrive at a place where we end up with a strange and familiar feeling affecting our entire being: "There must be something more." The reason for the feeling, which shakes us to our very core, ends up bringing us to the crux of our very existence. In our own humanness, we naturally gravitate toward self-sufficiency, and in doing so we make ourselves the key to the existence of the universe. Genesis 3 explains the reason for this. Because of Original Sin, God says, "The man has now become like one of us, knowing good and evil" (Genesis 3:22 NIV). Because of the fall, humanity becomes "godlike." Please note, in this context God uses the comparison with deep concern, which is very much opposite to the positive connotations associated with the phrase "Christlike."

On our own strength, humans climb, we reach new elevations, and we trample on those around us for our own personal advancement, because we are godlike. Notice how God does not say, "Man has become god." We are only like god. As fallen humans, we possess fragmented knowledge, and this knowledge pulls us toward a mirage displaying the self as master and king, as perfect and complete. Yet the harder we push toward the mirage, the more we endeavor to construct the self by satisfying the desires of self, the farther away the mirage moves.

Our godlikeness is really an innate pull toward our own self-sufficiency. We have the desire to stand alone, to use others for our own gain, and to do what is best for ourselves in a particular moment in time. All our realizations are constrained by time. We can see, but only dimly. We can perceive, but only partially. We can make judgments, but only incompletely. Our godlikeness gives us the desire to rule our own lives, but simultaneously leads us to our own destruction. With the fractured self at the center, the wagon wheel can never be fully complete. It will always possess the hub and the four spokes, but the felloes will be fractured or nonexistent.

The Wagon Wheel and the Redeemed Self

In the last chapter I discussed the first three chapters of Genesis. According to these passages, God created us for a reason, and when we become entangled in our own selfish desires, we can only ever travel down this road of purpose or that road of purpose, but we can never achieve a balance. And in doing so we can never rid ourselves of the subverted feeling telling us there is more to life than what we pursue.

Our origins, as discussed in Genesis, reveal an essential concept acting like a unifying gel in relation to our four purposes. Though God created the earth and placed man as the primary caretaker, and though he created the garden for Adam and Eve, God is still the central character. He created. He breathed life. He provides Adam and Eve with the garden. He speaks the instructions for humanity to follow. Even after the fall, he does not remove himself from what he created. Though he curses the ground with weeds, the ground continues to produce food. Though he increased the pains of childbearing, women continue to bear children. And though he banishes humanity from the garden, he continues to desire relationship with us. After Adam and Eve gain an awareness of their nakedness because of their sin, God makes it possible for them to remain in his presence by making clothes for them. God switches roles from universe creator to clothes designer. On initial appearances this is a menial task for a God so great and powerful, but at deeper level this task symbolizes of one of his deepest desires: to walk with humanity through their trials and through their search for meaning and purpose. Covering up

Adam and Eve's shame proves to be an act of grace allowing for a continuing relationship with the divine.

This desire denoted by the act of covering humanity so they might remain in his presence eventually translates into the ultimate act of sacrifice for Father God when he allows for his son to be sacrificed. His sacrifice not only provides us with an avenue into eternal life, but grants humanity access to walk with God in this finite world. Like God's creation of clothing to cover our shame in his presence, Christ's act on the cross, covers the shame of our sin and removes our guilt enabling humanity to discover our ultimate purpose: a life (and an eternity) spent in relationship with our Creator. Humanity's ultimate purpose cohesively connects each of our other four purposes.

The act of clothing ourselves with the redemption of Christ allows for one transformational event to take place in an individual's life. The person who's donned new garments does so with a new knowledge—the understanding that all they've toiled to achieve amounts to nothing when done for selfish motive. Christ's redeeming blood allows for God to become the center of our lives. An individual who accepts Christ's selfless act replaces their selfish core. Thus, we become willing to die to self in order to truly explore meaning and purpose. The only way an individual can arrive at an understanding of purpose is to choose not to be the focus of his or her own life.

What Christ says to Nicodemus in John 3, he also says to each one of us today regardless of celebrity status or wealth or fame. Anyone who comes to him, he requires them to die to self and to be born again. When Christ explains this to Nicodemus, he speaks of the rebirth as a mystery. He compares the work of the Holy Spirit to the wind as it "blows wherever it pleases" (John 3:8 NIV). In the same way the Holy Spirit restores and redeems the broken soul. And for what purpose? God's love for us. The same love which God reveals back in the garden when he expresses it is not good for man to be alone. The same love he shows to Adam and Eve when he creates clothes for them, so they can continue to walk with him. The same love he shows even when he curses the ground, in that he continues to allow it to bear fruit. The same love then transcends time to the point where Jesus predicts to Nicodemus God's sacrifice of his son, the ultimate act of sacrifice in order to achieve the restoration of humanity (John 3:14–15). It is only through Christ's act of restoration that we can experience wholeness.

We have to be willing to give up our lives. Only through our own sacrifice of self can we truly understand the self. Going back to the wagon wheel analogy, when we allow Christ to occupy the hub, he then restores the felloes as well. Each spoke connects to purpose, and each of the four purposes has no termination point. Work and creativity go from an avenue to build self, to a reformed direction in which a person glorifies God through his or her actions. Each spoke becomes a way to bring glory to God, and purpose extends from our selfless relationship with God. We no longer develop relationships with others so that we might gain from them; instead, we choose to give selflessly to honor God. When we rest, we do not make a god out of relaxation or entertainment, we simply see God as the author of rest. When we make moral choices, we do not place moral choice above our relationship with God. We make moral choices because we desire to honor God, and part of honoring him means we accept his grace and extend his grace to others. In essence, we recognize each spoke in and of itself as a fraction or a fragment of meaning needed in order to complement the other spokes and provide balance, and this balance can only be achieved by replacing the desire to be godlike, with the desire to become God's children. This could very well be humanity's primary tension.

The Redemption of God's Children

In light of becoming God's children, and no longer living our lives for selfish gain, we begin to see the world and those around us with renewed vision. Hansen, the student who viewed everything through his greatest strengths, which were hard work, intelligence, and drive, can begin to develop a full understanding of purpose. The students around him who were there so he could succeed, who he often looked down on for being less intelligent than he, now become individuals created by God who also possess strengths and weaknesses. When he sees the multiple facets of purpose, he no longer develops relationships for strategic or selfish reasons.

Along this trail, morality goes from an "ends-justifies-the-means philosophy," where gray areas are always used for personal advantage, to a simple desire to honor God. Hansen goes from wondering how to manipulate a moral code for personal gain to seeking God for wisdom in every situation. Wisdom becomes the starting point for difficult decision-making and not the moral line dividing right and wrong. In the same way he recognizes the need for rest, and honors God by resting and developing relationships through different avenues other than work. Essentially, God connects Hansen to a purposeful existence where he will never arrive at a crossroads in which he questions his reason for existing, regretting a life singularly focused on selfish gain.

And what about students like Tamera? What does life look like for her with a new understanding of purpose? Though she defends morality with good intentions, she continues to stand for what is right and good, but with God at the center (instead of herself), she goes from a shallow godlike interpretation of right and wrong, of good and evil, to a place where she is always willing to remember the grace God extended to her. She comes to a point where she sees self-righteousness is possibly humanity's most blinding fault. At this point she moves to a recognition where she understands that sinful living may be the opposite of moral behavior, but grace and forgiveness are the antidote to sin and guilt. Tamera removes herself from the judgment seat and allows the omniscient God who transcends time to take this place in her life. In doing so she frees herself from a burden she cannot bear. She begins to understand the context of morality, and she will begin to live a life of purpose, which situation can never steal from her. She will never arrive at a place where she feels betrayed by morality, because morality is no longer her identity, but a mere avenue through which she can glorify God, the author of every fiber of her being.

And what does a newly discovered understanding of purpose look like in a student like Aniston? She who singularly exists for relationships and who walks a treacherous path leading to destruction, where situation eventually robs her of purpose. She finds all her security in relationships and is most likely to crash the hardest because her entire identity, her entire purpose for living is deeply entangled in what others think of her. Life can be really good when relationships are good and life can be extremely bad when relationships are bad. Willing to sacrifice all for a friend or a boyfriend or girlfriend, the relational types solely rely on those around them for purpose. Aniston draws her feeling of connectedness from the well of relationship. However, by developing a deeper understanding of purpose, relationships develop a context. They go from the sole reason for existence to one of the reasons humans exist. Thus, when people disappoint, when relationships fall apart, when she wrongs someone, when a boyfriend puts her in a morally compromising situation, she can look at each of those situations and be affected (because we are all emotional beings who place trust in others) but not be shaken to her very core. For at her core, she no longer finds self and relationship, but God and deeper purpose.

When relationships break down, she can recover because she has a renewed confidence in Christ. When she finds herself in a questionable situation, she makes a positive moral choice because she desires to glorify God beyond her desire to find acceptance and love from her boyfriend. She gets off the path, the one where she arrives at forty years of age a broken individual, carrying relational burdens far too great for anyone to bear. Instead, she desires first to honor God. And in doing so she brings honor to herself and those she comes into contact with. She arrives at forty tested by life's trials, but ready to continue to face any challenge that comes her way, because she sees reason and purpose in the trials. Aniston has made mistakes, she has hurt others and been hurt by others, but whenever possible she seeks repair and forgiveness. She's been forgiven and she's forgiven herself. She does not carry burden or bitterness. She continues to desire life.

As for Joshua, with a renewed vision of purpose, he maybe gives up his dream to become a professional gamer. He begins to deal with the reason behind why he's gaming his life away—it could be an addiction or a bad pattern started when he was too naïve to recognize the dangers. Or maybe he has some deep hurt he's been avoiding all these years: something that happened at school or maybe the constant fighting between he and his parents. He begins to learn to put life into perspective, and sees that if he carries on with his entertainment overload, he will end up at forty sitting in the basement of his parent's house continuing to conquer levels but not able to achieve anything of consequence or importance. Joshua will at some point see that he's robbed himself of precious hours. He begins to see purpose in work and using his skills for God's glory. He begins to see relaxation and entertainment, not as a diversion, but as a way to rejuvenate one's body, mind and soul so as to be ready to give one's talents back to God. With God at the center of his being, a strong work ethic can actually add to the enjoyment Josh gets from relaxing. When he seeks this balance, he goes from godlike, or doing all he can to satisfy the self, to God's servant, doing all he can to glorify his creator. With God at the center, he removes himself from a path that ends in purposelessness; conversely, he places himself on a road where purpose exists each step of the way.

The Ultimate Challenge of the Redeemed Self

I can't say that once a person places Christ at the hub, life becomes a "happily-ever-after" scenario. In life we constantly face challenges and circumstances that don't make any sense. Life's storms that have the very real potential to erode an individual's trust in God, causing a person to seize control from him. To this point in my life, I've never been able to understand why certain difficulties and tragedies happen, but I'm moving to a point where I'm learning to trust that, though God may not orchestrate all situations in a fallen world, he has the ability to redeem every situation, if not in this life, then in the next. Thomas's story reminds me of this truth.

He is potentially the most misunderstood disciple. Anyone who's spent time under a steeple knows the adjective Christians use to describe Thomas. Presently, he's known by the masses as doubting Thomas, because he did not trust the report of the risen Messiah. In literature we'd call Thomas a flat character as opposed to a developed character. He's known for only one trait, which overshadows the rest of his personality. Does Christian culture arrive at this conclusion justly? In other words, does John's Gospel provide us with this information alone because it's all he knew of Thomas, or do we arrive at this understanding because humans naturally gravitate toward simplicity?

The answer to the Thomas riddle may be baffling, especially for those who've served Christ their entire lives. John actually provides attentive readers with more about Thomas's personality. He's not simply doubting Thomas. Conversely, he's fiercely loyal Thomas as well. He devoted his life to Christ and was willing to die for him. When Jesus speaks about going back to Judea because his good friend Lazarus was sick, some of the disciples warn him against taking the journey. They reminded him of a small issue that arose the last time they were in the region: the Jews tried to stone him. Unfazed, Jesus tells them his business is urgent. Lazarus has "fallen asleep" and he needs to go to "wake him up" (John 11:11 NIV). Some disciples, however, still did not see why they needed to head back into harm's way just to wake up an old friend, so Christ tells them plainly, without euphemism, his dear friend died. Christ needed to go to him so his Father could be glorified. When he makes it clear that he is going, regardless of personal danger, Thomas rallies the rest of the disciples by saying, "Let us also go, that we may die with Him" (John 11:16 NIV). Well before Thomas became doubting Thomas, he performed this action of bravery in support of his Rabbi. He knowingly placed himself in a deadly predicament in order to serve his Teacher. Thomas's loyalty runs deep, even to the point of ultimate personal harm.

A number of the very loyal people I know have something in common. It's difficult for them to understand a betrayer, because naturally they would walk to the ends of the earth for a friend. That said, most of us are egocentric; we initially assume all people think and feel the way we do. So a loyal person would only ever initially understand that a people around them would be loyal to the end as well. My guess then is that loyal Thomas felt extremely deeply about his rabbi and assumed correctly that Christ would be a person of his word and would be there until the end and would fulfill all his spoken promises. As Christ hung dying on the cross, according to Thomas, so did their relationship and all Christ had promised. A portion of loyal Thomas most likely died as well.

Motivated by this ground-shaking event, Thomas spoke the 28 words ultimately solidifying the negative one word adjective which now precedes his name, saying to the disciples who saw the risen Christ, "Unless I see the nail marks in his hands and put my finger where the nails were, and put my hand into his side, I will not believe" (John 20:25 NIV). I wonder if beneath the doubt he was also saying, "I'm deeply hurting because Christ said he would lead us to the end and now he's gone. I trusted that. I wanted that. I'm angry with myself because I couldn't protect him. I'm angry with him because he led me to assume no individual, no religious group, no legion could overpower him. And now ... now I'm left with nothing. So don't come in here and tell me the Rabbi, who I loved more fervently than any other person, is back, because my heart is so broken, so crushed, that it does not even possess enough space to hate you if you were lying to me."

Then an excruciating week passes.

Thomas and the others gather, holding onto remnants of a once tightknit group, and many believing Christ would once again appear. Some likely see themselves as more of a support group rather than what they formerly saw themselves as: a group with the potential to transform a culture. Then Christ enters the room, not through the door but through the wall. He's fully Spirit. But when he addresses Thomas, he reveals he's fully flesh as well. I imagine Thomas to be so emotionally confused he doesn't know whether to tackle Christ or embrace him. The Rabbi acknowledges the entire group and when he sees the loyal doubter he says, "Put your finger here; see my hands. Reach out your hand and put it into my side. Stop doubting and believe" (John 20:27 NIV). Presumably, Thomas reaches out and touches the Spirit's wounds expecting to feel nothing, but his finger physically circles each wound. With this complicated act, his loyalty resurfaces and he enthusiastically proclaims, "My Lord and my God!" (John 20:28 NIV).

I appreciate Thomas's story because I deeply identify with him. At times, I wonder how certain circumstances, hurt and scars could ever be redeemed. Events happen, like the death of a loved one or the destruction of a close relationship, that appear to be shrouded in finality, much like Thomas's assumption about Christ's death. This wondering and this doubt erode the felloes of my wagon wheel until I unconscientiously replace the redeemed self with the fractured self. But for me, hope exists in Thomas's narrative, which is really Christ's. It is a constant reminder that though I am a physical being living in a physical realm, I must never neglect the soul. For the soul is the connection point between the physical and the spiritual, between the temporal and the eternal.

Furthermore, because of what I know about Thomas and about Christ, I learn to trust that no circumstance is merely physical ... although I can only believe this if I believe in the cross. Because of God's desire to connect with humanity through his Son, hope is never lost. All can be redeemed.

PART 2

GOD'S WILL: AT THE HEART OF THE REDEEMED SELF

CHAPTER 5

A Big Misunderstanding

I'll never forget my old high school friend, Kent. He had such a strong desire to do God's will. In fact, he wanted to do God's will more than anything else in life. The only problem was that, according to Kent, God would not clearly tell him what to do. But he was strong willed, and he was willing to get tough with God. God *would* tell him what to do, and Kent *would* wait until God directed him before he made his first move.

Unfortunately, this faulty theological thought directed his life. He waited ... and waited ... and waited but God just would not tell him what to do. Until one day, Kent was driving down the road praying about what he was supposed to do after high school and ... God answered him? Right while he was in the middle of his prayer time an ambulance drove passed him on the way to a call.

Kent took that as a sign. Of course that is what God wanted him to do—become a paramedic. It only made sense, right? According to Kent it did because, for whatever reason this is how many of us in our school thought the will of God to be. If we waited on him long enough, if we dug in our heels and told God how serious we were, if we waited patiently enough, God would answer us and give us direction for the next stage of life.

With this type of faulty theology at the foundation of Kent's decision-making, of course the paramedic direction did not work out for him. He began to take courses to become an ambulance attendant, but realized after half a year that he really disliked most things associated with this line of work.

Obviously, this is an extreme example. Not all of my friends were as persistent or as literal as Kent, but in one way or another we still suffered from a misunderstanding of God's will. What I can't remember is how we adopted the misunderstanding on this deeply essential biblical issue, but what I do fully recognize now is where this line of thinking led me. It actually took me to a place of spiritual confusion. All I ever wanted to do was his will. And all I wanted in return was for God to give me assurance that I was doing his will. What drove me to a place of internal torment was that I thought I could know for certain. I realized that I needed to move forward in life, and I truly believed that once I finished university, and once I was in a career I would have no questions. I believed that if I was doing God's will I would be able to live a life of certainty and fulfillment, which is actually true, but not based on the understanding that I had. In my twenties I'd thought I'd solved the riddle of God's will, at least at a philosophical level. I believed that God's will for my life involved understanding what my greatest skills were, making those skills and gifts stronger, and then using them for his glory. It made perfect sense. So I moved forward and lived my life toward this end, thinking that once I accomplished, once I achieved, that is when I'd feel secure in his will. Though this thought helped me move forward, it still fell short of a full understanding of his will.

Fast-forward almost ten years and by the end of my twenties, I'd taken a job as a high school teacher in a private Christian school. I had the freedom to teach about Christ in the way that I deeply integrated biblical concepts into my daily lessons. On good days, I felt like I was making a difference, like I was doing his will for my life. But in the back of my mind, I had a nagging question—was I in the right career? Could God use me more in some other career? Should I become a pastor? Isn't that where God could use me the most? Did this question mean that he was calling me in this direction?

I'd battle these questions for months, and sometimes I'd even get to a point where I could envision making the transition into the church, leaving teaching behind forever. God, is that your will for me? I loved certain parts of teaching, and there were also parts of pastoring that looked very inviting to me. Was God calling me to stay or to go? To make matters worse, after six years of teaching, the church our school was affiliated with was seeking a discipleship pastor and they asked me if I'd be willing to consider the position. Was this God calling me to full-time church ministry?

All questions and no answers. I got to a place again where I felt like God would not answer me, and I felt betrayed. In the end I kept teaching and I felt, for my own sanity, I needed to focus completely on the vocation I was in. And it is here that I began to gain a new understanding of God's will. No more mental torture. No more being ineffective because I felt like I needed to be somewhere else. I began to explore the Scriptures in order to develop a new understanding of the question that plagued me the most: What does God want me to do with my life?

What's tragic is that so many Christians from my generation that I speak with can identify with me. Whenever I tell my story, people fire back with similar stories of bumbling about in search of God's will. And we're the ones parenting the next generation of God's children? So it makes perfect sense that when I listen to my students tell me about the confusion they feel about big decisions and pursuing God's will, I hear the exact same faulty theology that I had when I graduated. Similar to me at their age, many Christian teens truly believe that if they go to the right college and find the right spouse that they will find the peace of his will. The primary problem with thinking this way about God's will is that we are always chasing and never existing. When our youth, our children, believe they will be able to find God's will for their lives one day, somewhere out there in the future, they live a disillusion that has the potential to destroy their faith. God's will is not a destination. Yes, we desire to do God's will and seek his will. Equally though, we must be willing to exist in his will.

Last fall I led a group of students up a mountain in search of a downed WWII Lockheed P2V Bomber that crashed December of 1950. After much scrambling, we found the plane, or what was left of it. The crash site was like nothing I'd ever seen before. Millions of pieces everywhere: engines, propellers, wings, and the tail section. At the moment of impact, chaos, but now the pieces of plane rested peacefully, scattered over the multiple acre site where nine American servicemen lost their lives.

I'd heard rumors that the US government came to the site a few months after the crash and buried the guns and ammunition and collected the human remains. However, thoroughly completing these jobs was next to impossible because of the remoteness, the elevation, and sheer magnitude of the crash site. As a result, one of my students found the head of a fifty-caliber bullet and another student stumbled across half of a pelvic bone.

Looking out over the crash site, it appeared from the way the trees were sheered the plane flew straight into the mountain, which made me wonder why. A mountain is an obvious obstacle and not an object that's going to surprise an aviator. After much research when I arrived home from the hike, I discovered the probable reason for the crash. The crew of young servicemen was on a mission to search for a Russian submarine reportedly moving down Johnstone Strait. To complicate the next to already impossible mission, the bomber ran into thick fog causing the plane to veer off course and into the side of the mountain.

It's interesting because they were all on a mission, and they were doing it together. They all had jobs to do, and they all trusted that each member was able to do his job, but they still flew into the side of the mountain. This tragedy is very similar to the way the majority of Christians understand God's will at this time. We trust those around us (our pastors, our teachers, our mentors) to lead us in a way that will get us home safely, but because of our faulty understanding, we have veered off course. Our general understanding has us in a fog, but we move forward because we know nothing different. Sadly, we think we're on course, doing what's right, for the most righteous cause. But in truth, with our present perception of God's will, simply seeing I as an end goal rather than a present existence, our lives are going to become jumbled messes, with chaos reigning rather than the peace of God.

The plane wreck we're heading toward is easily avoided, but we have to be willing to look beyond our present understanding and begin to uncover a few simple Scriptural truths. We have to be willing to live in his known will, submit to his unknown will, and desire his all-encompassing will more than anything else in our lives. The Bible often discusses God's will, and at key times. In fact when Christ teaches us to pray, he makes known that we are to ask for God's will do be done on earth as well as in heaven (Matthew 6:10 NIV). And before Christ goes to make the ultimate sacrifice for us, for our sins, he prays that the cup of suffering and pain pass from him, but then he fully submits to the Father's plan of redemption for the human race, with the words, "But not my will but yours" (Luke 22:42 NIV). Because of Christ's sacrifice, we are able to exist in relationship with God. Because Christ bowed to God's will, we can exist in relationship with the Trinity. God made it possible, and most Christians desire to do God's will. The Word of God contains the key to a deeper understanding of his will for our lives, and once we become more cognizant of the different levels and dimensions of his will, we will begin to exist in his perfect plan and not feel like we are constantly fooling ourselves with mirages.

This may sound kind of odd, but we cannot spend our entire lives chasing what we can never know for certain. We can't spend the entirety of our beings wanting a concept that will always elude us. A person can only chase the pot of gold at the end of the rainbow for so long before they either give up all together or desire to know why, what they spent their whole lives chasing, did not exist. That is the point I came to. Chasing and pursuing constantly wore down my faith in Christ. Why would I want to strive my whole life, and not exist in Christ, in his love, in his peace, in his arms? My questioning brought me to a point where I had to choose between giving up (because I was spiritually exhausted and could go no farther) and questioning what I understood about God's will. I did the latter. What I found when I read through the Scriptures regarding God's will gave me an entirely new perspective on my faith and enabled me to not only carry on but to deepen my relationship with God.

One of the many problems with viewing God's will as completely unknown is that we treat God more like a fortuneteller or a genie granting us wishes. The issue with these two pictures is that a strong relationship is lacking—the fortune-teller concept works best if they do not know us (if they know us it's like they're cheating). God, on the other hand desires deep relationship with his creation. So as part of the design, we don't get to know outcomes up front. We must live our decisions in order to build trust in God's ultimate love. Certainty, in the moment when it comes to life's largest choices, actually is unrealistic and negates the need for trust. We can't ever know completely, but we can always trust completely. God, in his sovereignty, is more concerned about our ability to trust him than he is about our perceived need to experience a temporary comfort provided by the knowledge of an outcome. Certainty about outcome actually neutralizes the stimulation we find in the journey, and life has the potential to become boring when outcomes become too predictable.

So as parents, intensely desiring to invest in the lives of the children who follow us in the faith, we have an immense responsibility. God requires that we work with him in creating a new understanding of his will, creating a foundation so much more solid than the one that we built our futures on. Our challenge is to fight through the popular Christian opinion, a dangerous potion of shifting cultural truths mixed with elements of isolated portions of Scripture, and replace it with a new perception based solely on Scriptural teaching. The benefit is that the generation that follows will no longer have to muck about in search of a concept that does not exist, possibly stumbling upon the truth someday, or possibly missing it all together and giving up on the faith. If we are able teach them this new truth, this teaching will give them the opportunity to move beyond us, and begin to tackle other areas where God's people need to realign. What an exciting thought—that we get to be part of what he is doing!

It's time for us to revisit the Scriptures to explore what's said about his will. What we'll find is that more often than not when the New Testament authors discuss God's will, they discuss the known aspects of his will: the aspects encouraging us to deny our own selfish desires in pursuit of everything holy. A more biblical understanding of God's will instantly take us from a place of chasing to a place of daily living his will. His *known will* is that we love him with our entire being and that we love those we come into contact with more than we love ourselves. His known will is that we keep ourselves sexually pure. His known will reminds us to pray continually. His known will takes us from a point of cursing challenging circumstances to embracing them and being joyful in the midst of the storms because they drive us into the arms of Christ. His known will causes us to make a daily trek to the foot of the cross in search of forgiveness and grace and hope and love. His known will, through the power of his spirit, eventually becomes our will. For my friend Kent this means no more chasing ambulances, and for me, no more wondering if God could use me more somewhere else. It means our children pursue careers based on skill sets and the desires that God placed inside us. It means asking God to work through us in every experience we encounter throughout our days. Most importantly, it means experiencing God's peace in all circumstances.

CHAPTER 6

Teaching the Fullness of God's Will

Contrasting views have a tendency to make Christians feel uneasy. We naturally like concepts to be one way or the other, and sometimes they are. Like good and evil, even though multiple levels of complexity exist between the two opposites. But not all contrasts exist in polar extremes. Life is not that simple and this is part of God's design. Complexity creates mystery and creates a desire to pursue deeper truth, and has the potential to stave off cognitive and spiritual boredom.

Walt Whitman, one of America's most influential nineteenth century poets, in his poem "O Captain, My Captain" develops intensely contrasting moods within each stanza. The poem expresses both exaltation and sorrow. With adoration and pride, the speaker turns to share in the emotion of a successful journey with his captain. The ship is on its way into port, they have accomplished all that they have set out to accomplish and people line the shore to show their praise and gratitude for a job well done.

As the young man turns to share in the powerful moment with his captain, the person who's been responsible for the ship's success and who the multitudes are most excited to see, the speaker forcefully transitions to sorrow, for he sees his captain on the deck

"Fallen cold and dead."[12] The captain brought the crew through the storms and battles, all that they set out to accomplish has been successfully completed, but as the ship moves slowly toward its terminal point the captain falls to the deck and dies. He's lived long enough to complete the goals, but he cannot take part in the rejoicing and celebration that accompanies the completion of a large project.

And now, the speaker, the person with strong connection to the captain, looks upon the jubilant crowds and feels that he's been part of a monumental outcome, but the death of the captain also forces him to experience the deep emotion associated with monumental tragedy. These contrasting moods are balanced throughout the poem's three stanzas, with the poem's meaning found only in a full understanding of both existing together.

Like the poem, the New Testament is full of contrast which creates paradoxes and mysteries. For example, God's immense love for humanity contrasted with his inevitable judgment of the human race. Another contrast that's gone relatively unrecognized to this point in history is the balance between God's known will and his unknown will. Yet the fullness of his will can only be lived when we uncover the different dimensions that exist. God's will is both revealed and unrevealed, and in order for our children to live his will for the entirety of their lives, we need to teach them to fully understand of both aspects.

God's Unknown Will

The aspect that Christian teens gravitate toward is God's unknown will. They want to know the choices they make today will take them in the right direction in the future. Any time a crisis of choice exists, a person naturally desires certainty, and we falsely see God as an avenue that takes us in this direction. Young people want to know that the college they attend is the right college, and they want to know that the degree they are working hard to complete is the right one. They want to know that the person they might marry is going to be the one God has set aside for them.

It is correct for us to desire God's will in our lives, but a large divide exists between desiring and knowing. We can deeply desire God's will, but we must never believe that, in the moment, we can know with certainty his unknown will. We need to always be willing to move forward trusting that God's plan will unfold the way it is destined to unfold. When navigating through God's unknown will, we must do so in a way where we recognize our seeking is a desire for submission and not for personal advancement. Seeking God's direction for selfish gain can only lead to disappointment.

Numerous verses in the Bible discuss God's unknown will and how we should respond to it. First, Paul states that his calling is the result of God's will. He believes that he is "an apostle ... by the will of God" (Ephesians 1:1 NIV). Because we associate calling with God's will, which we rightly should, we assume that God calls us all to a specific vocation. But here Paul speaks of his destined salvation and his place in the church, which happens to be his vocation. And here is where it becomes important to not simply think that God called Paul in a *unique* way, so he is going to call all Christians in a unique way. That logically goes against the definition of the word *unique*. He may, but he most likely will not. That's what makes Paul's calling unique and noteworthy—not everyone is blinded and told in an audible voice what they should do with their lives.

What we can learn from Paul's calling, both to Christ and to his vocation, is that no matter what we end up doing with our lives, it is essential to not divide the two. We are called of Christ in every circumstance that we find ourselves in life. Christ calls us to share his love, grace, and salvation wherever we find ourselves, whether at work as a scientist in the lab, or as a forest technician out in the field. Unfortunately, what Christian young people take from events in the Scriptures, like Paul's calling as an apostle and Moses's calling to lead the people of Israel, is that they will also be called the same way: that God will speak to them in a similar fashion. And, once again, he may, but he most likely will not. God generally speaks to us differently today. Hebrews 1 says that in the past God spoke through prophets and forefathers, but "in these days he has spoken to us by His Son" (Hebrews 1:1–2 NIV). He speaks to us through the Scriptures, and he speaks to us quietly, in silence, and our responsibility is to take time to listen.

Our expectation then should be that God will direct us as we live and desire his will, not so much that he will tell us what to do with our futures. This mind shift alone takes the young person from a place of fear to a position of trust. God will guide me as I make God-honoring decisions, as opposed to what if I make the wrong decision and go in the wrong direction. The latter is paralyzing and the former is liberating. God is both omniscient and loving; therefore, if we desire to honor him with our entire lives, the decisions that we make will take us toward him. We do, however, live in a fallen world, so challenges, obstacles, and pain will be part of any path we travel. All success and failure on the trail we hike will be used in shaping the person God destined us to be.

Paul refers to God's unknown will in other ways as well, more than just calling. In Acts 18:21 Paul speaks to the Jews and they are moved by his words. He can't continue to stay and speak with them because he has to move on, so when they request that he stay, he declines and says, "If it is God's will, I will come back" (Acts 18:21 NIV). He reiterates these same comments in Romans 1 and in Romans 15. But take note of the way he makes reference to God's unknown will. He's not chasing after it like we so often do with comments like, "I just don't know what God's will for my life is." Instead, Paul submits to God's sovereignty. He's acknowledges God's full control of his life. Paul submits to the fact that God grants him breath and fully controls his timeline. His life is God's life, he's not using God as an excuse, and he's not desiring to know for certain that he will return. Paul makes a simple statement that places him under the God's control.

Similarly, James, brother of Christ, makes a point about future plans. He says that it's pointless to say tomorrow I will do this or become this … instead we must bow to God's sovereignty in our lives by acknowledging that we're not in control by stating, "If it is the Lord's will, we will live and do this or that" (James 4:15 NIV).

Part of submitting to God is acquiescing to the point that there's no possible way that we can know for certain the career we choose or the person we choose as a spouse is the right one. We can only trust that, when we step, we step forward in God's will. We move forward in the confidence that the trail we take won't lead to a dead end, but even if it does, God will sustain us, and not just sustain, but also use the time we spent hiking as part of his greater plan, whatever that might be. We can't move forward with full certainty in what the future holds for us, but we can move forward fully trusting our Creator.

In the ultimate act of submission, Christ goes to the cross in order to make salvation available for humanity. His commonly repeated prayer at Gethsemane is one in which he asks for the cup he has been served to pass from him. His desire is that he not go through what he knows is to come: the jeering, the torture, the pain, the agony, the exhaustion … the cross. He submits to his Father's will because he trusts in the Father's plan and purpose.

Near the end with his face to the ground, Christ pleads with God the Father. At the place near the Mount of Olives where he loved to pray, at Gethsemane the place which name means oil press, he submits to the plan—a plan in which he himself becomes like an olive, pressed and transformed into oil that the Father uses to create the Bread of Life, giving humanity the option to never go hungry again. At Gethsemane, Christ submits to the Father's will, and becomes a perfect example of what all Christ followers must learn to do.

When discussing the importance of trusting the sovereignty of God over our lives, I can't help but think of the challenge Indiana Jones faces just before he reaches the Grail in the *Last Crusade*. When he comes to a point in his pursuit to save his father's life and he's standing before, what appears to be a bottomless abyss with seemingly nowhere to walk across, Indiana makes the statement, "No one can cross this." Then he realizes that rationally, moving forward is an impossibility, he struggles to overcome the trust in his senses and rely solely on faith. He must trust that when he moves forward something unseen will catch his step and allow him to cross the void safely. Indiana places his hand on his chest, a universal sign that he's willing to take a leap of faith, and then takes the step forward. His foot finds a previously invisible bridge, and he's able to complete his quest.

In the same way, when we start out and face life's large decisions, we're unable to see beyond today. It's impossible to know what twists and turns and challenges await us as the result of the decisions that we make today. Every major decision essentially involves a leap of faith. We must have faith that what we pursue is part of Christ's perfect plan and results in us moving forward in God's will. All we can do is take the step—we can't connect the dots until we've lived our decision and we look back and realize that God truly does have his hand on the direction of our lives.

God's Known Will

As a summer job during my university days, I worked at a historic site and led education programs. While doing research in the archives one day, I stumbled across a story that so impressed me that it has not left me—even twenty years later. The real-life narrative had to do with the friendship and love between a schoolteacher, Adelaide Bailey, and the young man in her life, John Fingal Smith.

As the story goes, in the late 1800s Ms. Bailey took a teaching job in a remote and small community in southeast British Columbia. She bought a house and began teaching in the one-room schoolhouse. At some point she caught the eye of a young man who lived just down the road from her, and eventually the two began enjoying each other's company. After a time, John acquainted Adelaide with his feelings and his intentions toward her, but at that time in Canada, a female teacher could not be married and continue to hold her position—it was one or the other. She chose to remain faithful to John, but not to marry him, and to carry on with her teaching career.

Fingal Smith also remained a faithful friend all the years that Ms. Bailey taught. Not only did he remain faithful to his heart and his love for her, but he also maintained a strong relationship with Ms. Bailey. He did so by making her oatmeal every morning and bringing it over to her so that he could sit and have breakfast with her. After years of taking breakfast to Ms. Bailey, she finally retired from teaching at the age of 47, in 1905, and the two were finally able to get married. They remained faithful spouses to each other until death. In fact John Fingal Smith's epitaph reads: "A faithful lover for 18 years and a devoted husband for 31 years."

A bowl of oatmeal, deep commitment, and love for a lifetime. This story contains such a rich analogy for God's known will for our lives. Christian teens become so focused on the big picture that their attention is so easily diverted from the here and now, from the bowl of oatmeal. The big picture dreams, in order to become realized, need to be broken down into daily bowls of oatmeal, and Paul recognizes this in many of his teachings to the New Testament churches.

He discusses known aspects to God's will, aspects that allow the individual to take part in the day to day and not just in setting future plans. God communicates to Paul that a person can't have one without the other. Both must be present in order for a Christ follower to live God's will. God asks us to trust him to lead us in our future endeavors, and he reminds us that his will exists today. When large decisions face us, our focus on God's will becomes one dimensional, and can remain that way until we either go searching for a deeper understanding or we become disillusioned and give up. But the time of large decision-making is the most essential time to see the fullness of God's will, for the individual who neglects God's known will, ignores the peace that God provides even through the tough decision times.

God makes his known will extremely clear. He leaves us with very little guesswork. In Paul's first letter to the Thessalonian Church he reminds Christians God's will for them is to be sanctified and that they "should avoid sexual immorality" and "learn to control [their] own body in a way that is holy and honorable, not in passionate lust like the heathen who does not know God" (Thessalonians 4:3–5 NIV). In his final instructions, Paul further discloses what God's known will looks like. In chapter 5 he encourages the Thessalonians to be patient with one another, to ensure that nobody pays back a wrong for a wrong, and to, "Encourage the weak ... be joyful always; pray continually; give thanks in all circumstances" (Thessalonians 5:15–18 NIV). He also encourages the early Christians to "Test everything. Hold on to the good. Avoid every kind of evil" (Thessalonians 5:21–22 NIV).

Pastors and teachers often reference Romans 12 when discussing God's will but stop at verse 2, an indicator that most Christians erroneously believe that God's will is a complete mystery. So most Christians know that they can "Test and approve what God's will is" but do not connect to the end of chapter 11 which fully reminds us of God's sovereignty and his infinite wisdom, and we seldom realize that Paul carries on for the next few chapters in explaining what God's known will is for a believer.

He states that we should not think of ourselves highly so that we do not become isolated, self-serving individuals in a community that needs our contribution, but could function without us. Paul directs us to recognize that we have different gifts which should be used to build up the community God placed us in. He goes on to encourage the believer to love sincerely and hate evil practices; God's will is that we honor others above ourselves and that we keep our spiritual passion. Through God's power in our lives, we should endeavor to identify with those around us, to be excited with those who are excited and to empathize with those who mourn. Furthermore, God's will for the believer is to live in harmony with those around us, and not to be proud but to "be willing to associate with people in low position" (Romans 12:16 NIV).

God's known will draws us into community and allows for a sustainable community. Without forgiveness and patience, without recognition of the importance of others above self, a culture, a community quickly degenerates into individuals using a group for their own gain. In Mark 3, Christ states the importance of doing God's will. He says, " …whoever does God's will is [his] brother and sister and mother" (Mark 3:35 NIV). In other words, doing God's will ultimately creates relationship with Christ.

God's known will exists so that we're not simply chasing phantoms. The direction he provides through the Scriptures allows Christians to daily enjoy his presence and to make the most of a moment. Living God's will gives us day to day guidance so we're not chasing cultural truths that change as often as a new idea becomes popularized.

For example, through the '80s, messages coming from popular culture promoted gratuitous sexual activity outside of the confines of marriage. At the time, it seemed like the more people a person slept with the better off they were. However, in the late '80s people adhering to this cultural idea were forced to live with a new reality presented by a deeper understanding of sexually transmitted diseases (some life threatening).

Not long after the new reality presented itself, many of my friends lived in fear of society's updated message—reckless sex came with its consequences. Culture had to adjust to the new findings. In contrast, the truths present in the Scriptures gave peace to people who followed God's will, even in the face of outside pressure. God's will, though not always the easy route, provides individuals with insight that transcends public opinion. God's ways give believers vision beyond the here and now, and allow them to tap into wisdom beyond what would be naturally accessible to us. So in a paradoxical twist, God's known will provides the individual with deep insight into the future.

The Power of Understanding the Fullness of God's Will

"O Captain, My Captain," through the sorrow and the exultation expresses a deep truth about life—that tragedy exists when a person only focuses on the end goal, and it's equally tragic when a person no longer sees the need to work toward an end goal. Deep passion stays alive through a lifetime, like a smoldering coal in a campfire, only when a person recognizes the need to make the most of each day (in the essays and the math problems, the person that you bump into in the hallway and the time spent alone in contemplation) in balance with the end goal (working toward a degree and a career).

Whitman wrote this poem for former US President Abraham Lincoln after an assassin took the President's life as he watched a theatre production. Lincoln, instrumental in leading a country through a time of civil war, never got to see the country heal. He never had the opportunity to see the results of all he had worked hard to accomplish. He never had the chance to see the "people all exalting" for he'd fallen dead on the deck of the ship that he'd brought through dangerous waters.[13]

The theme of the poem relates to an essential aspect of God's will. His will for our lives is a balance between known and unknown, between living day to day and living with an end goal in mind, between working toward a dream and the completion of a dream. God communicates to us that life is made up of seconds, minutes, hours and days that he provides for us to desire him, and it is in those moments that we see God connecting dots into the shape he destined for us to be. The natural but self-serving desire to know what the shape is going to be before all the dots of life connect; this creates anxiety and paralysis in the moment. God asks that we trust the shape he's creating will be the best version of us. So regardless of whether we desire to honor God by becoming a pastor or a missionary, or a businessman or an electrician, we're using the skills given to us to glorify the One who gave them to us. We live God's will every moment so that we bring glory to him every moment.

I'll never forget the first time I stumbled upon a portion of this truth. The realization began to take root at my university graduation ceremony. A transformation happened somewhere between walking across the stage and sitting down. On the way back to my seat with degree in hand, a strange emptiness took the place of happiness like a thick fog moving through a city. All this time I'd worked toward this ceremony and receiving this paper, all this time I'd worked hard toward a dream of accomplishing this task, and now I sat down and thought, *So this is it. This is what it is like. All right, what's next?* At that moment, before I sent my mind into getting mentally lost in the next step, something made me back up and realize that each moment I'd spent accomplishing the task were equally as important as bringing the task through to completion. The friends I'd made along the way, the professors who'd invested in my life, the sacrifices my parents had made so that I could stand up on a stage and receive my degree, the late nights finishing assignments, and the later nights talking with friends about experiences we'd been through and about girls we were too afraid to ask out, desiring God's will in each of those moments was equally as important as the completion of the task. And more than that, eventually, in my mind, those moments became synonymous with the dream, not a separate part that made up the dream. What I didn't fully realize at the time was how closely these thoughts lined up with what the Bible teaches about the fullness of God's will.

CHAPTER 7

God's Will: More Important than the Breath I Breathe

I love Mr. Bean sketches. One of my favorite episodes is the one when he attends church. He shows up to a formal service, sits beside a stuffy church member, and then does anything but pay attention to what's going on. Bean fights to stay awake with constant head bobs and temporarily slumps onto the shoulder then lap of the stranger who's seated beside him. Eventually sleep fully takes over and he finds himself in an extremely awkward position on the floor. After he is startled awake, he wants to remain wide eyed, so he figures that putting a candy in his mouth will enable him to do so. The candy though is a hard candy with an extremely crinkly wrapper and every time he tries to open the wrapper, the man beside him shoots a disapproving look. The rest of the sketch has Mr. Bean trying to figure out how he's going to get that candy in his mouth without being noticed by the church member beside him. What makes the scene so humorous, in my mind, is that the church represents a concept of enormous gravity: salvation. Yet Bean is entirely consumed by boredom and begins to focus on a candy to divert his attention. Bean shows up to church, he's in the right place, but his focus has nothing to do with anything that's going on around him.

Really, our human nature drives us to the same point when we're forced to make a decision of immense gravity. Christians experience such tunnel vision that we become so consumed by the decision itself that the larger issue, our trust in God, becomes secondary to the process. The decision essentially becomes the candy that diverts our attention. We are consumed by a small reality when there's a larger reality that exists. Each year, usually a month or so into the semester, I ask my grade 12 classes the ultimate question: What is God's will for your life? Their answers all seem to have a similar thread running through them, and they all focus on the unknown path that lay ahead of them. God's will for many of them has everything to do with choices between two colleges. For others, they believe that God had not shown them his will yet, so they wait on God to reveal what he wants them to do. Still others have clear direction; usually these are the ones who are driven to become doctors, scientists or classical musicians. Clear direction is good, but unfortunately God's will only exists ahead of them. So I'll ask them, "But what about God's will, right now. What does he want from you?" The question catches them off guard, and I usually get a few humorous answers like "To sleep more," or "To eat as much pizza as I can at lunch time."

To use a parallel, we've conditioned our children to treat God's will like a kiss at the end of a romantic movie. Everything in the movie builds toward that kiss. You know the plot. Boy and girl like each other. They almost get together but something gets in the way. They get together and are happy but then the guy messes up and she leaves. But then she realizes that his mistake was just a misunderstanding so they get back together. Then they kiss while standing in front of a perfect sunset. All the focus builds toward this expression of love symbolic of the fact they are finally together. They've made the choice and they are moving forward. And this is the way that we treat God's will. All the tension exists because of the uncertainty. What should I choose? I can't decide. God help me do your will! But drawn into the tension of uncertainty, we forget that there's another sixty years (God willing) of living out that decision, and that's where God's known will comes into play. That's why the Bible discusses God's known will more than his unknown will, because we've got so many years of living out our decisions.

A Christian young person begins to develop an interest in God's will usually in their teens, when they become intrigued by life choices, when direction becomes uncertain, when they have to make weighty decisions that essentially establish their life course. The Christian teen develops an interest in God's unknown will because they must learn to trust that God will direct each foot step along life's path. But the fact that these kids are in their teens before they take any interest in God's will speaks so much to the concern that there is little to no teaching about the known concepts associated with God's will.

To deepen the discussion about God's will with my students, I end up providing them with an example and then asking them a question that they are unable to fit into their present understanding about God's direction for their lives. I use an example from the ministry, pastors to be exact, because in the students' minds, if anyone has an assured calling from God and a clear direction, then it has to be a pastor. But here is the problem that shakes the foundation of their understanding of God's will: *If a pastor has been called to go into the ministry, then they are doing God's will. True. What about a pastor who has a successful ministry? What if this same pastor is cheating on his wife with a member of the congregation or is abusing children who are under his trust and care? Is he still doing God's will?* This example allows students to think beyond simply a vocation or a calling. Entering into a career is just the starting point when it comes to doing God's will. God calls his followers to daily participate in his known will. So when we become a pastor, we avoid falling victim to sexual sins, and when we become an accountant, we see that we perform God's will by establishing a trustworthy reputation built on biblical truths. Understanding the interplay between God's known and unknown will, is an essential key to coming to realizing that what we do, quite possibly, might be less important than how we do it. We want to find ourselves entering into a career where we can fully develop and use the skills God placed in us, but if we do not conduct ourselves in a way that brings honor to God, then our skills become self-serving and not a gift to the one who created us.

Judas Iscariot opened up my eyes to this concept. For most of my life I knew what the majority of Christians knew about Judas's life: that he betrayed Christ. But for some reason, one day I decided that I did not like the fact that I looked at the betrayer in an immature and shallow way. He had to be more than that. The Bible had to provide more than this one fact about his life.

I began with the Gospels, books that I'd read so many times before, but this time I did so with Judas in mind. Every word that Jesus spoke, every miracle that he performed, every verbal trap set by the Pharisees that Christ turned into a teaching tool, every time Christ spoke and commanded nature's elements, I pictured Judas present, taking in the rarity and sheer awe of the event. Surely what he saw had to be like nothing he had ever seen before. Christ chose Judas, and now he had the opportunity to follow Christ. What a time to be alive!

I foolishly admit that, on more than one occasion, I've been jealous of the disciples. Christ personally called them. They *lived* with the Son of God. I've felt a little cheated at times because I have to read the accounts. I would much rather live the accounts. If only I could be there, then I wouldn't experience doubt. Right? I'd always desire him more than anything else in my life. Right? Not according to the actions of the disciples. Thomas doubted. Peter denied. Judas betrayed. Even the twelve he chose and who got to see it all, they had faith struggles. Why is this? Christ is the Son of God. So why would an individual who experiences all Christ has to offer, still turn away? For the longest time I'd always assumed that if I experienced the fullness of God's love, that I would have no choice but to love him. And in this statement I found the error. Judas betraying Christ after he has fully experienced Christ, in no way calls in to question the deity of Christ. It simply proves the reason for his existence here on earth. He came because he knew that we needed to be redeemed from darkness, from our fallen state.

Christ is God. He died for our sins, but we still have the "opportunity" to choose darkness over light, evil over righteousness, hate over love, and bitterness rather than forgiveness. Thus, Judas can be called by Christ and can experience fear when the boat that he is in is pounded by waves. He can feel his fear subside because the Christ that has called him has walked on water out to a boat and then calmed the seas (Mark 6). In fact, according to this passage, they had recently witnessed the miracle of Jesus feeding the 5,000 with limited bread and fish. But Mark says the disciples' "hearts were hardened" to the miracle (Mark 6:52 NIV). In other words, they didn't get it yet, that Christ was the Messiah. That he had the power to perform miracles, to speak to the wind, to walk on water, to heal the sick, to preach sermons that were divine in their essence and contained keys to understanding the kingdom of heaven. Initially, their hearts were hardened to the concept that they walked with the Son of God, the most influential human being ever to dirty his feet with earth's dust. At the time he fed the 5,000, they didn't understand that the blood that coursed through his veins was the same blood that would provide freedom for humanity.

It doesn't say for certain, but my guess is that sometime between here, and the other miracles and teachings, and the time that Judas betrays Christ with a kiss, that the betrayer acknowledges, along with Peter, that Jesus is the Christ. But at some point his calling means nothing. What he does, the person he is, the person whom Christ called him to become … they all mean nothing because Judas becomes transfixed by his temptation and his weakness. The power of darkness reveals itself fully in that the brightest of all light stands beside him and Judas still turns from Christ toward the pull of his own doubt, frustration, and selfish desire.

While Christ and the disciples spent time relaxing at the home of Simon the Leper, Mary comes to Christ and pours very expensive perfume over Christ's head. She is overcome by the presence of the Spirit and performs this act, motivated by unadulterated love and obedience. The disciples rebuke her because of the cost associated with the perfume and tell Mary of the foolishness of the action. They explain to her that all the money invested in the perfume could have gone to feeding the poor. "What a silly girl. She obviously does not know the heart of Christ like we do," you can almost hear them say. Then Christ weighs in on the debate and takes Mary's side. You see, normally the disciples would be right. They knew Christ's heart for the poor and disadvantaged, but here it's Mary that couldn't be more right because she's following a Spirit-led heart. It's here Christ reveals the near future to them, that he is not always going to be with them, that Mary has performed a beautiful act in preparing his body for burial. In the face of what seems right and what all present know the Messiah would want, in the face of what the disciples perceive Christ's will to be, Mary goes ahead and allows herself to be led by Christ's will for that moment.

Here's where it gets really interesting, because here is where we begin to see a clear difference between God's known will and his unknown will in Judas's life. Judas, who is a chosen disciple, who is doing what he's been called to do by Christ, leaves to betray the Messiah. Think about this. Judas is living his dream. All those years of wondering what he is going to do with the skills that he has and wondering how he is going to combine his two passions into a career, all that guessing dissipates when Christ comes along. Not only does he get to be a disciple of a cutting-edge teacher, he also gets to use his accounting skills in the process. He gets to be the money guy for Christ. This seems to be a perfect fit for him.

And herein we find the crux of the conundrum: when it comes to seeing God's will as only an unknown concept, we work toward that end and then once we achieve a major goal, we forget about his will. Judas is doing what Christ called him to do. He is following him. He is learning from him. He is doing his books for him. But somewhere throughout his time with Christ, Judas begins to stop living God's will. Judas stops living Christ's love. He ceases to die to self. He stops allowing Christ's teachings to penetrate his soul, and a gradual transition takes root in his life. He becomes consumed by his own selfish desires. His own thoughts of the way things should be become more important than the way Christ wants them to be, and he eventually see his life narrative as a story that he is going to write. Essentially, Judas stops living God's known will and starts to live for himself. He betrays the one who called him, and it's interesting that in Mark's account he does so directly after Christ condones what seems to be a money wasting action. Judas can't handle this. Jesus says that people all over the world through all different generations will remember her for this act, and then Judas "went to the chief priests to betray Jesus to them" (Mark 14:11 NIV).

Judas's story plays out in different ways and to a different extent today as well. I wish I had a week's holiday for every story I hear about ministers who end up leaving their calling and their families because they fall into affairs. I don't make this statement by way of judgment, because they're human and possess weaknesses just like the rest of us. I simply bring up this modern tragic hero because he chose to go into a profession where he takes a stand against sin and where he puts himself in a place to help others and to be Christ's servant. This type of behavior attracts people because, by very nature, this individual reflects Christ. He performs God's will and in doing so becomes attractive to those around him. A minister can allow others to mistake Christ's beauty for his own, and then take advantage of his flock.

If nothing else, this scenario (his last sermon which plays out in deed rather than in word) becomes a painful reminder that a Christian, beyond calling or career, is called by Christ to daily live his will by sacrificing and replacing human desire with his desire. Cursed we are by a fallen world, but blessed we are because of his grace, his forgiveness and his redemption. Christ provides a road map to follow, but he also provides us with tools to resume our journey once we've driven off the highway and become stuck in a roadside bog.

Which brings me back to Judas. He comes to a place where he fully recognizes what he's done. To that point in the betrayal of his rabbi, his potential savior, all he saw were dollar signs. Money motivated him to take the actions that he did. But in Matthew 27, after he sees his actions cost Christ far more than what Judas received, his thirty pieces of silver, he is seized with remorse. And I appreciate what he does next. He seeks forgiveness. Judas went to the chief priests and the elders and he declares, "I have sinned … for I have betrayed innocent blood" (Matthew 27:4 NIV). Here though we see that it is not enough to ask for forgiveness, we're required to seek forgiveness from the right place. Judas goes to the wrong location. He goes to the place where his selfish ambitions, his desire for money led him. As Jesus hung from the cross, he was establishing an alter where all of humanity has a place to go to unload their burden of sin. Think of how beautiful the story would have ended if Judas went to Christ as he hung from the cross, and he sought forgiveness there. The betrayer and the betrayed, the teacher and the disciple, the sinner and the divine, face-to-face and embodying the very reason for why he hung on that cross.

And what of Bean, how does he fit into the end of this chapter. In the middle of the church service he attends, the congregation sings the hymn *All Creatures of Our God and King*. Bean humorously fumbles through the sacred song, not knowing any words except for "hallelujah" in the chorus. Interestingly enough, the hymn is based on St. Francis of Assisi's song "Canticle of the Sun."

Through the verses St. Francis praises God for all he created, for the sun and moon, and the elements of the earth that sustain life. Near the end though, he expresses unusual gratitude to the Lord for what he calls, "sister Bodily Death." Strange. He praises God for death as well as all that sustains life. I would guess that he does so because he knows he has nothing to fear. The thirteenth-century saint sees death as a vehicle which brings him closer to God. He strongly cautions those who "die in mortal sin" but believes that "Happy those [Death] finds doing *Your most holy will*."[14] In other words, doing God's will—known and unknown—is more important than the breath we breathe.

CHAPTER 8

Our Responsibility Goes beyond Words

In one class a high-achieving student posed a number of questions to me. She said, "Mr. Bird, what's the point? Why do I need to bust my butt to get good grades? Is it just so I can get into a good university, so that I can get a good job, so that I can buy a nice house and nice cars? It all seems so shallow." Very perceptive. It made me wonder if this line of questions originated with what we model for our kids. Do our actions and the way we live, speak this message to our children. Undoubtedly, if this is the way we live, they do. Maybe we're saying the right things regarding God's will, but we're living an entirely different screenplay. Because of our own faulty understanding of his will, there is a good chance that if we've lived our lives desiring God's will at some point twenty years ago, when we were on our way to university or looking for a spouse, then there is a very real probability that we no longer even think about his will for our lives (unless we've experienced a major disruption). If this is true, then there is also a good chance that we're stuck in a place where life has become predictable and mechanical because we've taken all control away from God.

Tell me if this sounds familiar. You had big dreams and plans. Some things worked out the way that you wanted them too, but many did not. You continued to dream for a while, and after five or ten years, you even flirted with making some changes (finishing your Master's degree or switching careers), but now you have a wife or husband and kids for whom you're responsible. I get it. Tension exists between the idealistic dreams of youth and the way that life plays out. So instead of living your dreams, maybe you're bored with your reality, which is livable some of the time and survivable at other times. Any excitement that you experience has to do with the Starbucks coffee you pick up on Tuesdays and Fridays. You have a big house, a nice car, and a whole lot of debt that won't let you escape the confined box made of thick walls that you call the daily grind.

As a Christian stuck in a rut, we tend to forget that life with God connects us to a larger reality—a reality where our purpose is clear. It's in the day-in-day-out where we have to be willing to live his known will. When we don't, because of our human nature, we naturally place God in the copilot seat. We started out trusting him, but the everyday difficulties, the material distractions took us to a place where we control our relationship with God. The problem is that the two pronged leadership approach does not work with God. He leads. We follow. Period. In Matthew 6 he deals with this concept. Christ knows that, "Each day has enough trouble of its own" (Matthew 6:34 NIV). And he knows that our lives can become consumed by worrying about our needs, what we are going to eat for dinner and what we are going to wear to dinner to impress that boss who makes the decision on whether or not we get the promotion. Christ also makes it clear that the more we worry about those things, the more we're taking control of the situation, and the more we exclude him. He says that our heavenly Father is more than aware of our needs and that if we concern ourselves more with the needs than with loving him, then we are living life backward. Christ says, "Seek first His kingdom and His righteousness and all these things (our needs) will be given to [us] as well" (Matthew 6:33 NIV). The right order is of utmost importance. Our human nature says provide for yourself and your family and if you have time then fit God into your already too busy schedule. God's Word says pursue God first and he will make sure that we are taken care of. The first path leads to a troubled life of disillusionment and confusion, the second leads to a challenging life filled with joy and peace.

The relationship between Brutus and Cassius in Shakespeare's *Julius Caesar* provides a clear picture of the doomed double-leader approach. Cassius knows that the only way his plot to kill Caesar will be successful is if the highly respected Brutus is part of the conspiracy. Though Brutus is one of Caesar's most trusted friends, Cassius manipulates him to join in the treacherous plot. And even though the actual act of getting close to Caesar so that they can run their knives through him goes exactly as planned, what happens after is a disaster for the conspirators. Because of decisions that Brutus makes, the character that Cassius brings on board to secure public opinion, the plebeians turn against them and instead perceive them not as liberators but as butchers. Their response has everything to do with Brutus and Cassius and the fact that, though Cassius devises the plot, Brutus is the one that makes the decisions after the initial plot is executed. They seem to share leadership roles.

Cassius says that there is no way that Marcus Antony should be able to speak at Caesar's funeral, but the idealistic Brutus contradicts Cassius and says that a speech from Antony, under their guidance, will actually win them public favor. Antony goes to the pulpit after Brutus speaks, and ultimately destroys the conspirators' position through eloquence and sarcasm. Cassius proves to be right—they never should have let Antony speak.

With all the major decisions after this one, the two battle back and forth, both providing good reasons for the direction that they should go from the point they have arrived at, and ultimately Cassius always gives in to Brutus, which ends up leading to the demise of the conspirators. At a seemingly unimportant part of the plot, right before the Brutus's and Cassius's armies are to go to battle with the armies of Antony and Octavius, Brutus and Cassius *agree* for the first time since the inception of their murderous plot. The two agree on something that appears to be so trivial, but the fact that they both share an opinion is monumental. They are able to agree that they do not know how the day's battle will end but, "If we do meet again, we'll smile indeed;/If not, 'tis true this parting was well made."[15] Both echo this statement, and then Brutus concludes their dialogue here by making a simple (yet possibly profound) statement about the end of a day, stating that the events of the day and how they play out are uncertain, and all that is certain is that the day will end—and that information about the day is sufficient. True. The point Brutus makes actually involves a greater reality—that we are not in control, and that all we really can know about the future is that days will come and go whether or not we're part of them or not. In my opinion, we work so hard to control every aspect of our day, so that we have a false sense we truly are in control, but the harder we strive to lead (and put God in a place where we're comfortable with him) the more detached we become from our purpose and the more disillusioned we become with the reality that we've created for ourselves. The two-leader approach ultimately leads to a destructive end. It did with Brutus and Cassius, who end up ultimately losing their battles and then running on the same swords that they believed would provide them with freedom from what they perceived as tyranny.

This brings me back to my student's perceptive questions about why we work hard. If we do it for our own end, we will find some satisfaction and merit in this, especially if we evaluate its opposite. Where does laziness get us, and where does it lead a culture? Where does a poor education system or a lack of a standard education lead an individual or a culture? The truth is that even without a desire for God, a person can make an argument for the benefits of working hard in school, at university, at a career and at a marriage. The opposite can be full of obstacles and pitfalls. Going one step farther, though, and aligning ourselves with God creates a deeper sense of purpose and a greater reward system. We no longer do what we do for ourselves, and we no longer see ourselves as isolated individuals. All that we do becomes a sacrifice to our Creator. Our rewards are not simply possessions, but deeper relationship with God and with those around us. Doing all that we do for God's glory is our purpose and his will for us. So all of a sudden, a house is no longer an end goal, but a means for shelter in which we can be hospitable. A car is no longer a possession which reveals status, but a necessary means of transportation which enables us to be places that we can accomplish the tasks that God sets before us.

The good news is that, if you're willing, you can initially begin living God's will within your confined box you've created for yourself, because this box is more of a perception than a reality. It all starts with a desire to do God's known will. Through his strength, we can find joy in any circumstance, and not merely survive the situation until you can retire or win the lottery. Better news—once you begin to locate Christ's joy in your present situation, you'll begin to rely on Christ rather than self. He'll give you a fresh start, and you may begin to see your present situation as the exact place where you need to be to serve him, or Christ may give you the strength to move on, something which he's been calling you to do for all the years that you've been ignoring his voice. Where? The best part about living the full dimension of his will is that *where* matters less than your obedience. Your obedience will cultivate trust, and trust will cultivate a renewed love, and a renewed love will result in a clear path—a path that connects you to God, to the present, to the beauty that surrounds you. On this path you feel again. You experience God's love, your children's love, and your spouse's love. No longer do you merely exist, you live with purpose. And you begin to develop legacy that stretches beyond the paycheck you provide for your family. Your children see a person passionate about Christ, about his children and about life. You pass on a strong desire for the life God gives.

We see this progression in possibly one of the most entertaining conversations in the Old Testament, when Moses and God have a conversation about direction. God hears the suffering and the cries of his children and he's ready for them to move on to a better place. God gets Moses's attention with a burning bush and then proceeds to present Moses with his calling. He calls Moses to not just be a part of freeing an entire nation from slavery, but to actually lead them out of Egypt. Wow! God actually tells Moses exactly what he wants him to do. Most of us have desired that moment, and here it's happening to Moses. And maybe it's Moses's response that ruins it for the rest of us. Moses does not respond with a, "Yes! God finally told me what to do. Now I can go and live my life with certainty." Instead, he begins a series of questions and statements based on doubt and self-rejection.

God says go free my people, and initially Moses sounds humble in his reply. He says, "Who am I, that I should go to Pharaoh and bring the Israelites out of Egypt" (Exodus 3:11 NIV) I am no one. Thousands of other people could do a better job than I could. There are individuals who are far more educated, far more qualified, than I am. Sound familiar? How many times do we do that in life, when God calls us in a direction? We essentially say the same words as Moses: "Who am I?" But this is a subtle move to actually take control of a situation, to take the wheel away from God. When our responses are motived by self-rejection, we only ever envision the destination rather than the journey, but it's for the journey that God promises strength. God supplies what we lack. Seeing only the destination discounts the most important part of life, the day-to-day experiences and the people we meet along the way. We discount God's known will.

God responds to Moses's first question by stating he will be with him all the way through. Moses then says that suppose he does go, who should he say sent him? "I AM," God responds.

Moses asks a good question, but a few verses later his motive for asking the question comes out. Do I trust the "I AM"? How can I know that you will sustain me in my journey? This is going to be a tough one that I can't do alone, so what are you going to do to assure me that I can trust you? God essentially says to Moses, "You obey me and watch me work. I'll be the one to deal with the Egyptians." We've lost this—the ability to trust and in the process, we're passing along our self-sufficient Christian nature along to our children.

I've seen the Moses situation play out in my life as well. I worked hard to complete my education and establish a career, and trusted God through the process, because an element of the unknown always existed. But the longer I worked as a teacher, the more self-sufficient I became. My knowledge increased, so I knew what to expect from the students. My salary increased, so I could provide for my family. A strange thing happened the more comfortable I became with the life I'd built: I forgot what it was like to listen to God's voice, and I no longer allowed God to lead me. I became good at making excuses, so I could remain comfortable in what I'd established for myself and my family. I began to fit God into my plans, rather than aligning myself with his—and then I blamed God when life became dull and boring. I'd ignored God so many times that I knew only how to fit God into my plans, and God continued to call me to leave my self-sufficient life to serve him in a new way. I, like Moses, wanted to tend sheep, when God was calling me to step out and trust him. I asked the same questions: "Why me? Can I really trust you? What if I leave and all I want to do is go back?"

Moses carries on and tells the Lord about his shortcomings. Moses tells God that he can't speak very well, and God reminds Moses that he created him. When Moses is out of excuses, he finally asks God to go find someone else for the job. In this case though, no is not an acceptable answer to God. Moses must obey God, so Moses acquiesces to God's desire. An entire nation relies on this dialogue. And in our lives, though God gives us choice, no is not an acceptable answer either. An entire generation relies on our obedience to God. Our children *need* us to not just speak to them about God's will; they also need us to model a life of living out God's will. We can no longer afford to nonchalantly speak about the importance of living for God. We must live God with urgency. Since 2010, I've heard staggering statistics about the number of Christian children who fall away from their faith after high school (upward of 75 percent). Those who offer a solution say that the number one reason that our children fall away is intellectual skepticism and that the solution is to teach them more about apologetics. I do see validity in this solution, but all of the knowledge in the world won't save the next generation if what they see from us, their present leaders, is lip service. We can say that nothing in existence is more important than a life with Christ, but as parents we need to be willing to live like we believe the words we speak.

CHAPTER 9

The Pitfalls and the Successes

One day on our way home from school, my oldest son, who was in kindergarten at the time, asked the question, "My teacher says that God is a spirit, what does that mean?" My wife looked at me and with her eyes said, "This is your department honey." So I fumbled through an impromptu response about how God sent his Son, Jesus, to earth in human form, but now when we accept Christ, he comes and lives inside of us as spirit. I felt it to be an inadequate response, but it got the main idea across. Unfortunately, I used the word "spirit" again, so we were back to the question itself. I felt like a student asked to define a word and did so by simply using the word itself. This time though when I used the word "spirit" he made a connection. He said, "Like the fruit of the spirit." To which I said, "Yes, just like the fruit of the spirit." The car went silent for a few minutes. As I marveled over how I'd stumbled my way into facilitating a connection for my five-year-old son about the complexities of the Trinity, my three-year-old son broke the silence, and my proud teaching moment by saying, "You mean God's a fruit?"

Teaching theology to youngsters can be tricky, so it's no wonder along the way their understanding of a spiritual issue may need some tweaking. Regarding God's will, the importance of reminding our children to live God's will as well as pursue it is an essential proponent to their spiritual growth. Multiple hazards exist for children who carry on simply pursuing and never experiencing the peace that accompanies living God's will.

One of the most prominent problems is the issue of challenges and failure. If a teen's primary understanding is that they must simply work toward God's will, they are likely to view problems that occur on their way to accomplishing a goal as God closing a door. I believe that God does close doors, but I dislike the number of times that I see students using the "when God closes a door, he opens a window" cliché. Even though God does provide some opportunities while eliminating others, this saying is closely associated with the pursuit of God's will understood in isolation and not in correlation with practicing God's will. Some Christians erroneously believe that when we pursue God's will, everything will work out perfectly and no obstacles will present themselves. The main issue with this theory is that it's, um, completely false. The Bible teaches that we all live in a fallen world, and part of living in the fallen world is that troubles and difficulties constantly present themselves. Doing God's will in no way creates a force field around us making us immune from difficulties (Christ faced storms, Pharisees, traitors, betrayal, torture, and death), but it does allows us to experience peace in the middle of life's hurricanes. So why would everything work out perfectly? It is so important to teach our children to evaluate failure and challenges before interpreting them. We've created a Christian culture where our first response to rejection is to say, "God must be leading me in another direction." That's an example of interpreting. This may be the case, but we need to evaluate first. You might not get into a program at a college, but does that mean that every college that offers the program will reject you? A good question to ask is why did you get rejected? One common reason that students do not get into a program is because of their grades. So are you willing to bring up your English mark (which coincidently you slept through most classes your previous year in high school because it was first block and you always stayed up too late gaming)? A disconnect exists. Is God directing that student away from the program, or is there a lesson to be learned in consequences and a way to rectify the problem of low grades? If we have pure motives to glorify God in all that we accomplish, a strong desire to succeed in a certain field, and a skill set that we have and are willing to cultivate, then there is a good chance that is a career in which you can glorify God. Our first response, rather than to give up on a direction, should be to evaluate motive and work ethic. What caused this rejection? Are there other steps I can take so I have a better chance at success? Life takes a great amount of endurance, willingness to work, and tackling difficult choices where one must place deep faith in God. Those who embrace this concept have the opportunity to see God at work. And as a result, develop a deeper trust in their greatest relationship.

I've heard of far too many Christian students who went on to college or university and came across a novel that they felt morally questionable, so they withdrew from the course or university all together because they believed that God was closing a door. This is interesting, because they were usually the same students who firmly believed that God called them to the program. So God was wrong? Or did they just not hear God's voice properly?

Challenges and moral complexities exist all the way along to accomplishing goals. Christians say they live in a fallen world, but I don't know if they always believe it. The goals that we pursue will be fraught with failures and challenges. Rather than assuming God must be calling a person in a different direction, we should be teaching our children that challenges are one way God's children are forced to make the choice between relying on self or trusting him. Is there a way that we could get around the reading of a morally questionable novel and bring glory to God in the process? Is it possible to read the novel with a critical mind and then do an assignment where the student evaluates the novel from a Christian worldview?

My first year at college, I'll never forget the novel one of my English professors required his students to read. The novel took much artistic license with the biblical flood account, and presented what I believed to be sacrilegious material. The God character was old and powerless, and one of the most disgusting scenes included an odd form of bestiality. My professor thoroughly enjoyed the book and made a number of references to the positive spiritual content included in the book.

One of my friends dropped the course because of the novel, but I decided to take a different approach. I went to my professor and asked if I could write an essay comparing the biblical flood account to the account presented in the novel. He thought that was a fantastic idea, so I set about restudying the Genesis account and constructed strong arguments that contradicted many points the professor had taught the class about the subject.

A few weeks after the assignment due date, I was studying in the library and was situated close enough to a few people that I could not help but overhear their conversation. It turned out they were in a different block of the same course with the same professor, and they discussed a paper he handed out in class that day which compared the biblical account of the flood to the novel. After a few minutes of listening in on their conversation, my curiosity got the better of me, and I turned and asked if I could see the paper they were talking about. They handed me my essay. It turned out he had distributed my essay to all his classes (except for the one I was in). So as near as I could figure, about 150 students got to read an essay that contrasted the novel's description of the flood with the actual account.

The problem with dropping out or changing directions every time we're faced with difficult circumstances is that we never have to trust God—that God can make good out of bad situations, that God has a better outcome for those who love him. I know circumstances exist where an individual must take a moral stand, but I also know that God can use Christians in challenging situations to bring about his peace and purpose. Let's mature to a point where we can prayerfully decipher between the two. So when one of our children comes to us and says that they feel like they want to change directions, it might be good to ask a few questions. Do they want to change directions because of the challenges that exist? If so, it would be good to remind them that challenges exist in every avenue of life and ask them if they've prayed for strength and a measure of endurance to overcome the challenge and see the task through to the end. Remind them of other obstacles they've overcome and the feelings associated with being an overcomer.

Sometimes, a bump in the road is simply the last problem in a line of issues. Ask if other pressures exist as well causing them to want to change directions. Often, when a young person feels like they need to change direction, it's because they are experiencing multiple pressures, and they feel overwhelmed by their present circumstance. God gives strength to those in need, and he can help them through. Pressure-filled circumstances can be a time where we can lean heavily on God and be reminded of God's faithfulness. So the question then becomes, Does God want you to change directions or is he bringing you to a place where you need to recognize that you can't do it alone and you need to rely on God and those around you for help? More and more, I believe that challenges and difficulties are God's call to trust rather than a call away from present circumstances. If we're constantly trying to decipher God's unknown will, then we always have an excuse to move in another direction when the trail becomes too tough to travel alone. We can quit, but the other option is to acknowledge one of life's most counterintuitive truths—that we're not designed to travel alone.

Motive and God's Will

I'm not a huge fan of shows like *X Factor* and *American Idol*. Every once in a while near the start of a season I'll tune in though, just to get a laugh. I especially appreciate the people who try out for the show who have little to no talent. For fear of sounding naïve, I do wonder how much of the "no talent" is actually staged and how much is truly a lack of ability. But it does touch on an interesting issue—why would someone who has no talent, say as a singer, show up for a singing competition? Lots of variables exist but I think what causes people to show up and try out probably has everything to do with motive mixed with an inability to estimate their own skills (which is actually difficult for most young people).

In relation to God's will and his direction, one of the greatest factors involved driving an individual is perceived skill. For a person of faith, we believe that God gave us certain gifts and skills so that we can use them to glorify him, both in our careers and in an edification of the body of Christ. Motivation can cause us to misuse our talents or cause an individual to go in an entirely wrong direction. People motivated singularly by fame, for example, have a good chance of ending up in a place where they don't have a skill set to match their circumstance—thus *American Idol* humor. The viewer benefits from a person displaying their singing inability, exchanging their pride for seconds of instantaneous, yet extremely fleeting, fame. I realize that this is an extreme example, but in it contains a general truth in relation to God's will of which Christians should be cognizant. Pure, Christ-centered motives lead us in a God honoring direction. Selfish motives do not. Motivators like fame, wealth, revenge, and power (to name a few) should be flagged and shelved. And as Christians, we need to be extremely mindful when it comes to using God for selfish gain. Christ talks about this toward the end of the Sermon on the Mount. He acknowledges that, even when it comes to God, people can have misguided intensions. Some people may use

God for their own selfish gain. Christ points out that many will come to him and say, "Lord, Lord, did we not prophesy in your name, and in your name drive out demons and perform miracles?" (Matthew 7:22 NIV). He will disown them for using his name for selfish gain. A very sobering thought, that humans have the capacity to perform activities with God on their minds, but not in their hearts—completely unacceptable in God's eyes. What is acceptable? Christ states clearly, only the person who does "the will of my Father who is in heaven" (Matthew 7:21 NIV) is permitted entry into an eternity with Father God. According to this passage, God's will has everything to do with the fruit that we produce in our lives. For only a good tree can produce good fruit. In other words, God's will is not necessarily the actions we perform, but the actions we perform are an indicator of our obedience to God and his work in our lives. It's the difference between building forts around tree trunks, as opposed to being branches that shoot out of the trunk. Both require the trunk of a tree, but one is man-made and gets in the way of the tree's natural beauty and the other is the tree the way it's designed to be.

In my elementary years, my brothers and I had an unsafe two-story tree fort that we felt needed to be demolished. My older brother chose my father's crowbar as his demolition weapon. The destruction process proceeded quite well until we faced our first board, which happened to be one that we originally secured with so many nails to ensure it stayed in place. We strategically positioned this two by six as a guardrail on the roof so that no one could fall off the top of the fort and inevitably break something. From our mother, we'd heard a lot about potential injuries, but most had to do with people getting hit in the eye.

Now, as my older brother struggled to remove the safety rail, he not only dislodged the well-fastened board, he somehow dislodged himself from the roof. As the rail sprung free of the tree, no guard existed from keeping my brother from beginning his unexpected fifteen-foot decent to the hard ground. Fortunately, for my brother, he grabbed a branch to stop his free fall. Unfortunately, he projected off the top with such force that his body over rotated and the hand that held the branch could hold no more when his wrist snapped like a twig. He fell the rest of the way to the ground and was completely lucky that he did not lose an eye, but unlucky in the sense that he landed on the safety board used to prevent people from falling. Like a dying antagonist from a cheesy '80s action film, he slowly rose to his feet with the board fixed to his side. It appeared like every single one of those nails pierced his side. With a frustrated look on his face, he pushed the board off himself and began to limp to the door of the house, my mother now alerted and in full panic mode. The day ended in an emergency room.

Which is really where we should start ... in full recognition that we're injured and in full need of our divine physician and savior. If we start here, then really there will be less of a chance of us mucking around at the base of trees building and destroying tree forts. This seems to be the metaphor Christ discusses in Matthew 7. His discussion requires us to ask ourselves if we're going to be part of the tree-fort building crew, or if we're going to be part of the tree itself. One way leads to life of full submission to his will. Only then will we be able to produce good fruit that is pleasing to the Father. The opposite is prevalent amongst Christians who are unwilling to let God take control of their lives. We build tree forts around the trees that Christ invites us to be part of, and we do it in the name of Christ, but we build because we're not willing to fully trust him with our lives. To the tree-fort builders, the Father says, depart from me. I never knew you. Trust me or don't trust me, but don't pretend—you're only injuring my name. Our motives must be pure.

Pure Motives Lead to Using Talents for God's Glory

When it comes to skills and talents, our children can also be either tree-fort builders or be part of the vine. Those who build tree forts are the ones who experience a disconnect between motive and talents. They don't really care what skills God has gifted them with; instead, they start with an end goal in mind. For example, I want to be famous, so what careers can I go into where I can achieve this goal. Another may want to hoard as much wealth as possible, so they look for careers that will make provide them with excess wealth. Starting with a goal that does not glorify God and then trying to fit God into your project may work for a short time (meaning a lifetime) but will not play out well for the long term (meaning eternity).

Our responsibility as people who have influence over the next generation is to encourage them not to start with an end goal in mind, but with what God has given to them. He has given them skills and talents which they can use to not only serve their Creator, but that they can also use to create a good living which they can find fulfillment in. The biggest challenge for us as mentors is a recognition that helping our children locate talents is not always as simple as, "Oh, you're good at this so you should think about going in this direction or that direction." By the end of high school a student may or may not have developed an understanding of what skills they possess. They may feel like they have nothing to offer, or conversely, they may have a number of skills and not know what direction they can choose that would enable them to make full use of their skills.

To further complicate matters, some children are late bloomers in certain skill areas. For five years, between the ages of five and ten, one player in my son's soccer league dominated the pitch. Whatever team he played on, won the majority of their games that season. Now at 12, this same young man is barely noticeable on the pitch. Why? He was better than the others and maybe he felt like he didn't need to work hard, or maybe as kids get older the game becomes more strategic and the kids become more skilled so it's harder for an individual to play as an individual: they need to start trusting their teammates.

In the classroom a teacher sees this as well. Some students are good at a subject and are good all through their high school years, while others, for whatever reason, may not be able to meet the requirements later on. Kids who write well when they are younger may lose interest later on in high school, or vice versa. Some kids who could not write very well in junior high, find a series of novels they love, so they now have a strong desire to become a more accomplished writer. The same can happen with math, or with science or French. Some students change, while others stay the same. Students can carry the messages of a teacher or a parent for a lifetime. Messages like "Jonny you are such a good writer, so you should become a journalist," or "Angela, you should really become a teacher because you are so good at helping your fellow students understand this material." The opposite is true as well. Students hold on to the negative messages maybe even more than the positive ones. "Jimmy, I can't wait until you're finished this course—you'll never be able to understand the importance of the written word." Because Jimmy has limited self-awareness, he is impeded by that belief in all areas of his life and carries that around as baggage. Wherever he goes, those words hang in the back of his mind, until he has enough life experience to realize that a life focused on limiting beliefs is actually no life at all. With all the factors, and all the messages teens receive from mass media and social media, and with all the messages those around them speak into their lives (some true and others not true, often both taken to heart) the prospects of finding a career and a spouse can be daunting, leaving an individual paralyzed with fear about the next move after high school.

Our role, when it comes to their skills and talents, should be more that of a coach rather than a cheerleader. The cheerleader, with pompoms in hand, utters clichéd phrases like "you can do anything you want to do," or "you're the best no matter what." Though these phrases may build a child up temporarily, at some point they will recognize that maybe they can do whatever they want to do with their lives, but they may not be able to find fulfillment or satisfaction in doing just anything. It's much more beneficial to take on the role of coach in this area. As a coach, you take what they possess, and you encourage them to do something with their skills. You give them parameters, and you know when to be an encourager and when to push them by telling them the truth in love: that they may need to work harder, or set higher standards, or that it's their attitude that's getting in the way of them accomplishing all that they can accomplish. It's essential as parents to fill this role before their grade 12 year. Be this person all through high school. If you jump into the role when they have to make the big decision, then you have not built relationship capacity in this area, and they may tune you out (although it's never too late to try, you just may have to be more persistent.) When your son or daughter is making their big directional decision, that's the Final Four, the World Series, the Super Bowl, and the Stanley Cup, all mixed into one. You never just jump in and begin coaching at that point.

The parable of the talents in Matthew 25 contains an intersection of all that's been discussed. The passage reveals the perfect balance between God's involvement and our responsibility when it comes to the skills we have. The word *talent* and the way that we understand it today, is actually taken from this parable. Originally the word represented a monetary unit, but because of this parable and the truths associated with it, the English language uses the word *talent* to mean natural skills or gifts that one has.

One of the first lessons that we learn from this passage is that God gives us our talents. And thus, as Christians, we are reminded the skills we possess are not our own. What we do with our abilities should never be for selfish gain. Our talents are actually a responsibility—we are responsible to use them for God's glory, to furthering his kingdom. That which he has given to us, there comes a time where we must give it back. We see this with the servants the master entrusted with his wealth. Two go out and use what they have to gain more. When the master comes back, the two servants who gained more with what they were given, end up being praised by the master and then being given more responsibility, and invited to share in their master's happiness.

Their success breeds more success and a deeper favor in the master's eyes. The formula here seems to be quite simple. Take what has been given to you and go confidently and do the most that you can with it. When you've finished doing all that you can, give it back to the God who gave it to you, and then you will be greatly rewarded. The reward goes beyond simply using your skills for God's glory, which in and of itself contains the treasure associated with a job well done. God's reward system has some type of a positive snowball effect. Use what you've been given, give it back, and watch as your responsibilities and your blessings grow. In this light, helping our children move in a successful direction seems so much less daunting—simple, use your skills for God's glory. Interestingly enough, in the parable the master gives little to no instruction as to what he wants from his servants. He gives them what they need and then he expects them to know what to do with it. This actually seems a lot like what he does with the skills he's given to us. It's actually the servant who thinks too much about what he's supposed to do that gets himself into trouble.

The servant who's built the least amount of trust with his master focuses not on what he's been given but on a perceived understanding of his master, which causes him fear. The servant says to his master, you are a hard man and you take from places where you have not spread seed. So operating on this assumption, the servant says, "I was *afraid* and went out and hid your talent in the ground ..." (Matthew 25:25 NIV). Then he proceeds to give his unused talent back to his master. Back to motivation, his action is driven by fear of what the master might do. What we learn from this part of the parable is that two possible tragic outcomes exist when it comes to the skills that God entrusts us with. The first tragedy happens when we, as more of an observer, assume we know what God wants. What he wants is relationship driven by love and trust, not a servant who is constantly second guessing his master. So when we sit back and nonchalantly talk about God, and sometimes fit him into our schedule, and try to make him adapt to our selfish desires, then we end up making false assumptions about God. The second tragedy happens when we try to overthink the situation and then choose not to use our talent at all—when we bury it. We protect it in the name of the Father, but our talents are not designed to be guarded. God designed them to be fully used. The two servants who are in tune with the heart of God go "at once" (Matthew 25:16 NIV) to do what the master desired. They go with their master's purpose connected to their purpose. However, the servant who digs a hole in the ground "went off" under a false assumption created from his lack of truly understanding the master.

In an oddly paradoxical way, this parable can actually create fear in the hearts of the readers (it did in me for a period of time). What if I don't use my skills in the greatest way possible? Am I going to get punished? Should I become a pastor or an English teacher? But to think this way is to actually miss the entire point of the parable which is if we love and understand our master, and we desire to use what he has given to us for his glory, then in no way are we squandering the talents he entrusted to us. We are doing his will and utilizing our talents. Head in a direction with a desire to honor him, be faithful to him along the way, and he will make our paths straight.

Eliminating the Guessing Game

When it comes to God's unknown will, it's not that he doesn't answer when we call out to him, it's just that he does not answer the way that we desire—with an audible voice telling us the path that he wants us on for the time being. He's provided us with just what we need to get started, not too much so that we become bored with life or bored with him. He gives us just enough so that we can take a step, fully trusting God that the direction we're going is *with* him (not so much toward him). I think that may be where the mind shift needs to take place. When we're making plans, we want to know that the direction we're headed in takes us toward Christ. There's error in this thought though. For Christ is not really a direction or a destination, he indwells us. He's with us. So we don't need to chase after him, we need to experience him. There's freedom in that thought, that with Christ in us, the direction we go Christ will be there because he is in us guiding us and we are there.

Author of *Paradise Lost*, one of the greatest accomplishments of the English Literature tradition, John Milton, went blind at age forty-six. In his sonnet "On His Blindness" the narrator grapples with the challenges of a person who's talented in the area of writing but can no longer see and thus feels he can no longer write. Alluding to the Parable of the Talents, the speaker questions God as to what to do with "That one talent which is death to hide …" Is he forgiven if he does not use it now that he feels like it's impossible to use it? In a frustrated, and somewhat accusatory tone, the speaker says, "What now?" What should I do now that I can't do what you've created me to do? Like a Pharisee, he's got a riddle that doesn't seem to fit into the teachings in the Gospels, and he challenges God to come up with a solution. God, am I still responsible? Then in the sestet (the last six lines) the mood changes from a person asking this question: Does God require me to use my skills for his glory "light denied"?[16] to a person broken and humbled by the recognition that "God does not need / Either man's work or his own gifts."[17] The person that God uses is the person who desires to serve him. Those "who best / bear his mild yoke, they serve him best."[18]

In other words, rest in the knowledge that if you choose to serve the Creator, you will serve him. Avoid getting caught up in the dangers of the "What does God want me to do?" guessing game. Desire to serve him and then look for an opportunity to do so and you will. Just this morning I received a Facebook message from a parent saying their son was in tears last night as they filled out Bible College forms in preparation for next year. Through his raw emotion he echoed that he was not sure that this was the direction that God wanted him to go; furthermore, he was not even assured of his salvation. How sad that our students, our children, come to this place. God is not the author of confusion, so why do our children feel so much confusion at this time? Through what they've picked up to this point, they've got part of it right—the part where they want to do God's will and go in a direction that he desires of them. The next part, the going with God as opposed to searching and seeking, is the missing part of the equation. The desire mixed with the assurance he will guide as we walk with him, that's what will allow our children to step out in confidence and in peace.

PART 3

FREEDOM, RESPONSIBILITY, AND REDISCOVERING THE CORE OF THE CHRISTIAN FAITH

CHAPTER 10

Learning to Walk the Ridge

Last fall I visited Niagara Falls for the first time in my life. Growing up, I'd seen pictures and read about the history of the area, and now at forty-one, I peered over the Canadian side of the falls in utter awe. There I was, with tourists from all over the world, my iPhone held high recording the immense power of the moment. Later I found out that the falls attract more than just visitors; they can be a draw for adventure seekers as well. Numerous funambulists walked rope across the gorge, some even did laundry, ate lunch, and performed the stunt with an individual on their shoulders. Most recently, in 2012, an individual performed a daredevil act at the location: he was another tightrope walker who successfully walked closer to the actual falls than anyone has done in history.

People have also swam the rapids below the falls, swam the river from the American side to the Canadian side, and have even plunged over the falls in a barrel—though not all lived to tell their story or gain fame from their experience. The second person to go over the falls, and the first male, Bobby Leech, negotiated the falls in a barrel in 1911. He lived to make some money and notoriety from his stunt but sustained multiple fractures and lacerations and had to spend a period of time in the hospital after the event.

Leech performed the stunt in a metal barrel with a harness and a hammock on the inside to secure him. He touted himself as the "first man" to perform the harrowing act, which was true, because a sixty-one-year-old female schoolteacher had shot over the falls in a barrel ten years earlier. For years after the successful feat, Leech traveled around Canada, the United States, and even New Zealand speaking about the topic. About fifteen years after the calculated barrel stunt, he gave a lecture in Christchurch, New Zealand that would be his last. After this talk, the great death-defying man met his demise, and not the way you might expect a daredevil to go. Leech slipped on a carelessly discarded orange peel and broke his leg. With strange irony at work, he developed gangrene in his leg and died while having his leg amputated.

Leech lived the 167-foot drop over Niagara Falls in a metal barrel yet died of complications after slipping on an orange peel? A banana peel maybe, but an orange peel? I don't really know of anybody that has ever said, "When I go, I want it to be an orange peel that gets me. That's the way to go." Life can be random and crazy. We have little control over certain events that happen in our lives. In the '70s, a health enthusiast died from drinking too much carrot juice, another person died while asleep when a cow fell though his roof and onto his bed, still another lady died of water intoxication after drinking large amounts of liquid without urinating in an effort to win a radio contest.

So much information exists about the random and the unusual that the world must be governed by chaos. Right? Well, not really. Chaos and irony exist, and to be sure, media agencies will always capitalize on events that catch the public off guard. So the sensational and the unusual, that's what often makes the news. People desire the unique; they want to know life is more than the same old *Groundhog Day*, repeating over and over again. And in culture's desire to escape the mundane, we can so easily forget that checks and balances exist, that opposites exist in life creating an equilibrium holding the chaos to the periphery. Some accidents are truly accidents and have very little explanation or reason as to why they happened, but we can prevent most accidents by paying attention to common sense and possessing a certain level of situational awareness.

I've spent the majority of my life in faith communities (schools, universities, churches), so I've seen this same concept happen there repeatedly as well. Instead of unusual events, Christians (individuals and institutions) can end up sidetracked by polarizing subjects. When this happens, we can let the poles define us instead of the median. It's not uncommon for faith communities to gravitate toward perceived polar opposites, especially in the area of freedom and responsibility.

Like our culture's draw to the unusual, faith communities can easily and unknowingly gravitate toward the outskirts, and begin emphasizing fringe aspects of faith over the core elements of the faith. Central faith issues can become ignored in an effort to engage members who already "know" everything there is to know about the essence of faith. As the metaphor goes, we can get tied up in the stories about people meeting their demise on an orange peel or dying because of an overindulgence of water in an effort to win a contest. No doubt, the unusual, baffling, and conflicting aspects of the Scriptures exist, but we have to be careful not to make them central. Translation errors, predestination discussions, millennial talks, Paul's thorn in his side, the role of Tongues in the Christian life, all these are interesting topics that we can have opinions about, but they must be viewed as secondary topics. A rousing Bible study discussion is good, but in some way, unless the discussion connects to raw faith, the discussion has the potential to become self-serving. And self-edifying faith discussions have the potential to initiate a slow march toward the trivial. When this happens, the study of Scripture becomes a distorted. Scripture morphs into sledgehammer used to win arguments, to prove others wrong, and to beat others down and to oppress them. This tone seems to be more common in denominations that emphasize responsibility over freedom.

On the flip side, some faith groups tout their deep desire to separate themselves from the stuffy and traditional, or those groups who neglect freedom in Christ in favor of their responsibility to him. They don't want to present the persona of the stereotypical North American, white-haired, suit-wearing, tie-sporting, Scripture-spouting churchgoer. They present a false air of isolated freedom, with little recognition that the individual has any type of scriptural standard to adhere to.

Newer generations of North American Christians generally view our faith through the telescope of individual freedom. We are nearly exclusively concerned with our personal relationship. How is my prayer life? What should I ask for in prayer? What can I receive from Christ? How did the sermon affect me today? How does the church I attend suit me? What is Christ doing in my life? I'm not saying that personal is not important. What I am saying is that self finds more importance within a larger context. We've created a situation where we exist at the center of the universe, and although we are important to God and he finds value in us, our relationship with him is more than a self-help project. If it was, then we might as well have Tony Robbins come and speak on Sunday morning. The church for all its faults, for all its dressed up ladies who self-righteously judge every situation around them and look down their noses at the less fortunate, for all the old grumpy men who find more importance in telling others that they are wrong rather than walking beside a young person and mentoring them in wisdom, for every person who walks out because the music does not minister to them, the church is a community where a Christ follower is called to unselfishly invest. Yet in a desire to emphasize individual freedom, this believer neglects raw faith, and the concept of Christ calling an individual to lose their life in order to gain life.

As parents of the next generation, we should be wary of teaching our children to view freedom and responsibility as opposites, at least in the traditional sense. The Scriptures teach elements of freedom in walking with Christ, and they also teach an element of responsibility. In a situation like this, where opposites are both represented, there is a good chance that they exist because of a call to maintain a healthy tension. Am I free to eat this food? Yes. As an adult, am I free to drink this wine? Yes. But be responsible about it. Make sure that you do so in moderation and don't cause those around you to stumble (1 Corinthians 10:23–33). A pull exists here. In Christ you are free, but be responsible with your freedom. At the mid point of the rubber band being stretched in different directions, this is where raw faith exists. This is where we must be selflessly invested in Christ who gives us strength to live within this healthy tension, as opposed to giving in to one side or the other. At the median, this is where the believer experiences peace in Christ.

It's not uncommon for our children to envision freedom and responsibility as two separate peaks. You can only ever climb one or the other, because of the large valley between the two. We treat the two concepts like polar opposites, when in reality, within the Scriptures the two exist as partners, as complements. The two are not separate peaks with a large trench in between but are the same mountain ridge that must be negotiated in order to reach the peak. On the one side, falling headlong into freedom creates narcissism and libertarianism, and on the other side tumbling into responsibility creates rigidity and legalism. The ridge comprised of the two is the same ridge that we are responsible for in teaching our children to successfully negotiate, thus enabling them to avoid self-imposed chaos.

Generally speaking, our children are drawn to unfettered freedom, but this has its pitfalls. Freedom without parameters eventually ends up becoming its true opposite—confinement. Individual freedom, whether cultural or spiritual, when not paired with responsibility can only result in a downward trajectory. And I'm afraid within the church, generally we've been not necessarily overtly condoning, but passively allowing individual freedom to exist without balance, thus producing a Christian generation hypersensitive to individual rights but with little understanding of their responsibility to community. Freedom alone produces an egocentric child; whereas, responsibility alone engenders oppression and a deep desire to escape from the present situation. As parents, through our teaching or lack of teaching, we've painted detailed self-portraits of our children, so the individual recognizes how important they are to God, and to their family unit, but we've neglected placing them within the community landscape.

Perhaps in our efforts to weld cultural philosophies with scriptural truths, we've cultivated individual pods, individual barrels for ourselves. How else are we to plunge safely over life's waterfalls? How else are we to draw attention to ourselves? Christ though, does not teach that we are to preserve our lives; he teaches quite the opposite, that we must lose our lives in order to truly experience life. Our lives are not to be about ourselves; they are to be about him. Here exists the crossroads. We strive so hard to create a faith that suits us, a barrel that has all the comforts that life can afford us. Christ though already created a faith path for us to follow. It's just that we have to be willing to let go of all selfish desire in order to truly experience freedom. The individual is not an isolated leaf on life's tree, but an essential component of the strength and vitality of its entirety. Teaching our children this idea may go against every cultural message that bombards them, but it may just be part of a solution that allows them to experience true and eternal life.

In the midst of running around aimlessly, endeavoring to keep up with popular messages and trendy theology, it might be a good idea to revisit the fiber creating the rope that the two heavyweights, freedom and responsibility, use in their tug-o-warring battle. It's time to revisit raw faith with our kids. And raw faith at its very core requires the individual to reach beyond the self.

CHAPTER 11

Our Language as an Indicator

When it comes to working with teens, I'm on the front lines. I interact with them every day, for better or worse. The classroom presents its own challenges, but the overcrowded hallways are where the real excitement happens during the day. When I enter the corridors of higher education during breaks and lunch, acrid smells and over exuberant noises assault the senses. Between classes, the hallway instantly becomes an eclectic mix of grade 8 body odor intermingling with the wafts of a grade 10 boy who uses excessive amounts of cologne in hopes the cheap knockoff he's doused himself with is enough to attract that special young lady sitting across the English classroom from him during second block.

The grade 11 and 12s fall into two camps. There are the ones whose senses have deadened over the years, so they make no comment to the younger crowd creating the stench. Or they may fall into the other camp that has made it their mission to tell each and every student who adds to the putridity of break time to make sure that they take advantage of the daily shower routine or that cologne is not meant to be smelled by girls a continent away—nor is it meant as a replacement for the shower.

If one can get past the smell of the overcrowded hallway, it's the ears that take the second assault like a roundhouse kick to the side of the head. Teens yelling to one another over the already loud drone of all the voices excited just to be free from class even for a few minutes. Teenage boys cause a boisterous commotion while trying to steal a sandwich from a friend or trying to get the attention of a young lady who can't seem to hear a word he says so he speaks even louder, not realizing that volume has nothing to do with her not hearing him. Other girls quickly form a group after class and begin giggling and shrieking and then go quiet just long enough for the cute guy to amble by.

Some might call the high school hallway a workplace hazard, but I am used to this environment. One becomes somewhat desensitized to the buzz and the pungent odor, but every once in a while something happens that awakens the abused senses from their calloused state. On one particular day a few years ago, a student used God's name, which should not be anything abnormal in a Christian school. But in this case it cut through the air like Peter's sword on a soldier's ear. The young lady flippantly used God's name in vain as part of a phrase. I continued to walk along in disbelief telling myself that the student must have used another word that sounded similar, and I had simply misheard her. But then a few days later I heard it again from her, and a few days after that I walked into my class and heard it again from another student before the bell rang to start the block. At that point, I went to the students who I'd originally heard use his name in a careless manner and spoke with them. Then I began to address all my classes on the topic of using God's name in such a careless manner.

The responses I got when I addressed the topic fascinated me. Some student recognized the seriousness of using God's name so purposelessly, while others did not see the problem with using his name in such a way. One student said, "It's just a phrase and not a big deal. Everyone uses it." Truth be told, I have noticed it more lately, Christian students using God's name in vain, without purpose and without intention. I know that words lose meaning, and words that were awful to use in my day don't really have too much bite left to them nowadays. I understand that, but I think this is different, and I think we have to take this as an indicator, not necessarily that the whole Christian sky is falling but more that we have to be more intentional about training the next generation to recognize the seriousness of the journey they're on and how imperative our language is to that journey. As parents, we have to be more deliberate in teaching them their faith requires them to adhere to a higher standard along the road of personal discipleship. I firmly believe that a student who does use God's name without intent, who uses it as part of a meaningless expression, is the same student who also does not recognize that there is power in his name.

Our language ebbs and flows; some words carry power one day and then disappear a few years later. Some words become a trademark for a generation as they grow, but then the same word spoken by the same people may just indicate they're trying to hold on to a time that really was only great in their minds. Some words convey emotion while others create an emotion. Swear words, for example, generally come from a few different sources like bodily functions, body parts, sexual acts, or religious names or terms. It's not hard to figure out why names of body parts, bodily functions, and sexual acts become common fodder for crude names and words that a person uses to express offense, displeasure, or anger. A swear word takes its power from the fact that it's taboo because it originates from a socially unacceptable subject. I recognize that swear words can be thrown around carelessly, but generally they originally have purpose behind them. A youngster may want to exude an evil appearance, so they start using the word; a mill worker may want to appear free of any form of high society, so he chooses to use words that may repulse a certain portion of the population. The point is that originally a person uses the words because the words have the power to offend. So how do religious curse words make their way into the language? They can also be taboo in many situations, but they also have the added bonus of claiming inherent power in the mere mention of the name, and can express offense to a large people group who believes that there is power in the name.

To add to the use of swear words and curse words, one must also recognize that language is passed along from generation to generation. Words may be used by one generation in a specific situation for a specific purpose and then be used by the children of the next generation. But the children may only end up understanding context and not original meaning or purpose. Thus, you can have an entire group of young people using God's name in vain without specific intention. They heard their parents say it when they missed an easy scoring chance in soccer, so they say it when they miss a scoring chance. The phrase eventually becomes an expression of emotion with little recognition of original meaning.

Some words or phrases evolve to a point where culture uses them, but we have no idea where they originated. Take *to kick the bucket*, for example. Most of us know what that means; it means to die. It's really an insensitive way to say that someone or something no longer exists. A person may use it to show that they have no emotional connection to the person who's passed away. Or maybe a couple's feline died. The lady, who loved the cat dearly because it understood her and listened to her without trying to fix her problems, might say that she *lost* her soul mate. Meanwhile, her husband, who never listened, is happy that the cat finally died because now his wife may actually pay a little attention to him. He might say to a friend that the cat finally *kicked the bucket*. A reason exists as to why we use different words in different situations even though they might have the identical dictionary definition. The phrase *kick the bucket* came out of an era where public execution, particularly hanging, was common. To kick the bucket meant

Lost Teens, Lost Faith

that the executioner came along and knocked over the bucket an offender stood on; thus, causing a person to hang from the rope and die. That would be the reason this phrase is an impersonal way to say that a person died. Most people watching the execution probably had very little emotional connection to the person being hung.

The Liberal and the Legalist

I know I really need to be careful here because I am taking a small issue and elevating it. But please bear with me as I develop my point. My intention is to address the heart of the issue and what it says about understanding the deeper issue in play. I don't believe that a teen who uses God's name carelessly is on the road to a questionable future or is going to fall away from God, but what I'd like to do is address my concerns about what this trend indicates without relying on extremes. It's so easy to take a topic to an extreme. And when I speak with others about this particular issue, I try to avoid allowing others to take it there as well. For when the issue goes polar, we miss the heart of the matter. The liberal and the legalist are fun to listen to when it comes to debating faith issues, but on this issue they can up end up in a very similar place.

The liberal says, "Lighten up; it's no big deal to use God's name that way. It's just a meaningless cultural saying. My faith allows me to be free in what comes out of my mouth. If I'm always thinking about what comes out of my mouth, then I'm not going to be able to concentrate on looking for opportunities to tell my friends about Christ. And besides, the Bible says not to judge people—it's not like I'm going to hell if I take God's name in vain." The legalist, on the other hand, can provide the liberal with every chapter and verse proving that, yes in fact, he will be going to hell if he does irreverently speak God's name.

121

"It's not like I'm going to hell if I ..." and "You're going to hell if you ..." Whenever people use these phrases, it's like the trump card is out. How do you argue with this? The phrase makes me cringe though. Not because I do not believe in heaven and hell, but because I don't think one person's judgment of another person's eternal destination has any place in our faith. God alone judges us. When the liberal and the legalist talk about the fires of Gehenna, one uses the phrase as justification and the other as condemnation, and both miss the heart of the matter. They miss out on the importance of the eighty years or so that we walk through life on earth by simply fast forwarding to the end. What does this generation of Christian teens using this word indicate about themselves and about those of us who've raised them?

The Importance of Words

The Bible, specifically the Old Testament, has many names for God. In our culture, though, we generally refer to Father God as God. We use a descriptor, an adjective, to make his name more personal, and uppercase *G* to set him apart from lesser gods. Because really, the word *God* originally was more of a description of what he is, that which is to be worshiped. Now though in our Christian culture, we use his name *God* to mean the one, true God. The name *God* today refers the God of the Bible, personal and loving, yet who will one day judge the earth. The Hebrews used the word Eloheim to mean God. They also used the word *Adonai*, meaning the Lord, because Jewish scribes would not write nor pronounce the name of God 'YHAH' out of reverence for him and his name. They did not want to pronounce it for fear of using it in vain (Exodus 20:7) nor write it for fear that they would write it and it would be erased. His name comes from Exodus 3 in his conversation with Moses when he asks God who he should say sent him to deliver the Israelites from Egypt. God responds by saying, "Tell them I AM sent you" (Exodus 3:14 NIV). Tell them that pure existence, and original existence sent you.

It's interesting that we can go from a group of people in the Old Testament, with such reverence and utter awe for God that they came up with a different name for God because his name is so sacred, to a place thousands of years after the writing of the New Testament in a Christian school where we study and serve the same God, that some students would think it fine not only to say the name of God, but also use his name as a key component in a meaningless cultural expression. In a way, it's like finding a word that represents the biggest discovery of all time and includes all future discoveries (a cure for cancer, the invention of the computer, automobiles, rockets, cameras …) and then diminishing the word by constantly using it in a phrase that denoted surprise, or disgust, or any emotion or lack thereof that you wanted it to. Has everything changed so much over the course of history that even a concept as big as God, as astronomical as the creator of the universe, as grandiose as raw existence, as pervasive as salvation, means nothing? Should we ever leave a place where God's name is not exulted and glorified, where we no longer treat his name with knee-bowing, jaw-dropping respect?

Our language is a key indicator of what is going on in our hearts, and if our children are using God's name in a flippant manner there's a good chance they also see his involvement in their lives as relatively trivial. In Matthew 12, Christ has an encounter with the Pharisees where he exposes their hearts by challenging the language they speak. Most Pharisees despised Christ. He could not do anything without them testing him or questioning his motives and his power. What they couldn't do was to question his actions, so they looked for ways to discredit him. In the first Gospel, Matthew describes one particular Jesus/Pharisee run-in shortly after Christ healed a demon-possessed man who could not speak or see. Those who saw the miracle stood amazed, but the Pharisees, who could not explain away the miracle, attributed

Christ's power to Satan. It is only by "the prince of demons that this fellow drives out demons," they said (Matthew 12:24 NIV). When Christ hears their preposterous statement, he uses it as a teaching tool to bring the conversation back to the realm of truth. Jesus reminds them that a kingdom divided against itself is the same kingdom that crumbles. A kingdom at odds with itself will surely come to ruins. Christ says the Pharisees' accusations reveal who they are inside. In this case their diction indicates deep knowledge yet a spiritually dead heart. They know all about God's power, yet they do not experience his power.

Christ speaks with frankness so as to leave no room for confusion. He says the words that come from their mouths indicate the person they are. They are not divided against themselves. The words they speak indicate the core of what exists. Then through metaphor he says a tree is recognized by its fruit. A good tree cannot produce bad fruit and a bad tree cannot produce good fruit. The two are one in the same. We cannot escape our own words and can only communicate what is on our hearts. Christ calls the Pharisees a "brood of vipers," a group of deadly snakes, and then asks them a rhetorical question: "How can you who are evil say anything good? For out of the overflow of the heart the mouth speaks" (Matthew 12:34 NIV). Christ goes on to explain that everyone will be held responsible for the careless words they've spoken. Our words are so closely tied to who we are that Christ says our words will either set us free or condemn us (Matthew 12:37 NIV).

The words we speak to others, to ourselves, to God, they tell the story of our hearts. Carelessly using God's name speaks volumes. A Christian using his name in vain reveals that he or she has possibly lost touch with God's power and the spiritual significance of what takes place around us and our role in all that goes on around us. We may not only lack self-awareness but a spiritual awareness; we may be dull to the significance of a word and a name: a name that created the universe through words. In possibly one of the best on screen father/son relationship moments, I'm reminded of the importance of a name and how a single name can tie to something so much bigger than ourselves.

In one of the pivotal scenes in *Indiana Jones: The Last Crusade* (undoubtedly the best of the four), Indiana and his father Dr. Jones narrowly escape the Nazis in a motorcycle and sidecar. Throughout the escape scene Indiana surprises himself on a number of occasions. Once by grabbing a flag pole and using it as a jousting lance to overcome a Nazi motorcyclist and then shoving the same pole through the front wheel spokes of another Nazi rider and launching him like a catapult would a stone. Throughout the scene Dr. Jones shows very little emotion except for annoyance and even in the aftermath of Indiana's heroic motorcycle feats, Dr. Jones does little more than nonchalantly check his pocket watch. The only time Indiana gets a reaction from him is when, after they've left the Nazi captors behind, they come to a crossroads and Dr. Jones lets his son know he's going the wrong way. With a sign showing Venice one way and Berlin the other, Dr. Jones tells Indiana that they have to go back into danger; they have to go back toward Berlin to retrieve his diary that the Nazis stole. Indiana puts up a fight and says they don't have to go back for his father's diary because Marcus (a friend) already has the map that will take them to the Holy Grail. Dr. Jones says there is more in the diary than just the map, that the diary contains the secret instructions revealing how to get past the deadly traps protecting the Grail. When Dr. Jones says Marcus would agree with him about risking their lives to go back for the diary, Indiana disapprovingly responds, "Two selfless martyrs ..."[19] Then, with a perturbed tone, he takes Christ's name in vain. Indiana's use of Christ's name in this way results in Dr. Jones slapping him across the face, and responding, "That's for blasphemy."[20] Then he goes on to explain the essence of their journey. He says, "The quest for the Grail is not archeology. It's a race against evil. If it is captured by the Nazis, the armies of darkness will march all over the face of the earth ..."[21]

Similarly, the road that we travel is more than getting from one point to the next. What goes on is far more than all that's apparent to an individual in a moment. It's so easy to forget, even as a Christ follower, that there's more than what appears right in front of us. According to pastor and theologian Dietrich Bonhoeffer (who had life-long struggles with the Nazis, which ended in his execution), "There is meaning in every journey that is unknown to the traveler." Our words connect to a deeper reality. Words can hurt and heal, create life and enact death, and determine our eternal destiny. Like Dr. Jones, we have to peer beyond the natural and the physical.

People curse using God's name because it's more than just a name, and the minute we say his name is fine to use in a meaningless cultural phrase, is the same minute we lose recognition of the personal relationship, the sovereignty, the power, the holiness, the love, the desire, the omniscience, and the everlasting. Words we speak should be connected to meaningful thought. I used to do an exercise with my Bible class where I'd randomly ring a bell and then ask them to write down the thought at that precise moment in class. Looking back it may have been a dangerous project, but it always proved to be entertaining. At the end of this particular lesson, I'd ask for the thoughts to be handed in, and during the next class I'd read through the more entertaining ones. The teenage boys were normally quite predictable. Some thought about food, some thought about the girl across the classroom, and others thought about gaming. The girls often thought about who they were going to hang out with after school and what they were going to talk about. Less often than I'd hoped for, a student's answer indicated they grappled with the day's Bible lesson. I'd hoped for 100 percent mental involvement and definitely did not get it. It proved my point though.

The next day we'd talk about thoughts, particularly the amount of time we spend thinking about God or calling on God during the day. Though a few people throughout history have tried to think only on God, I don't know if that is possible or a necessary goal. I drew attention to how little time we spend thinking about God during the day. The students were in Bible class with a teacher speaking to them about God, and they had trouble maintaining focus on him through that time period. It can be difficult even when we're in an environment conducive to thoughts of God to focus on him, never mind when we find ourselves in nonconducive circumstances.

The students mentally engaged with the concept and often asked questions like "How much should I think about God during the day?" I emphasized the point that it is not how much we should think about him because this leads to legalistic thinking. The point is not *how much*; it's not numbers or time. The question is how do we make God central in our lives. How do we live the greatest commandment: "Love the Lord your God with all your heart and with all your soul and with all your mind" (Matthew 22:37 NIV)? That's the starting point. This is what it comes to. We can go back to the third commandment and state that we should not state God's name in vain, but Christ says that all the Law hangs on the greatest commandment.

If we love God with our entire beings, then amount becomes secondary to love. How much time? Not really relevant, because all we do, the words that we speak, our intentions, our desires, become entwined with what he's doing in us. We call on God through each moment and each hour because we desire more wisdom, because we recognize every good gift comes from God, because we know every challenge has the potential to bring glory to God, and because we know God has the ability to bring peace to every situation. Our journey becomes a journey toward and for God.

The crux, the central point, may not be the way we're willing to use God's name, the epicenter in a discussion of language is that language gives shape to an individual's thoughts and their thoughts stem from the heart, the very soul of an individual. So the language we use indicates whether or not we understand the true meaning of the journey. For Dr. Jones, he comprehends the weight of their success. In fact, failure is not an option, because if they fail, then evil wins, and he is not going to let that happen. We also have to recognize interconnectedness of what we do. We have to understand that our lives are more than a series of events all amounting to the jeans we buy and whether or not we look good in them. Our lives amount to more than the makeup we put on in the morning and the fashionable shoes that speak volumes about us. If we make our lives all about ourselves, then our language—both nonverbal and verbal—can't help but scream that fact. So how do we get our kids to speak a different language than culture speaks? This just might be the best question we can ask ourselves if we are willing to look deep into the words coming out of their mouths, and understand their hearts are at stake. For it is the heart, that's what Christ wants. Take care of the heart, and the words that come from the mouth will follow.

My concern is what our generation of parents models for our kids when it comes to conversation. If you are anything like me, I know I can fall into an unhealthy pattern modeling anything but what I want my kids and students to be passionate about when it comes to their faith. When I look back, I can see long periods exist in my time as a father and spiritual mentor where I should be the last person leading my children or other people's children. As embarrassed as I am to admit it, I've gone through times where I've display a mechanical and stale faith. I am supposed to be leading my family; supposed to be the Dr. Jones figuratively slapping my kids in the face when their mouths reveal they've lost sight of what is at stake, and reminding them our decisions, our responses, our actions interconnect and can change the course of history. But I've been the exact opposite, at times treating the journey like I'm just an isolated member trying to make it by. I'm just a cultural robot tying to pay down a mortgage, make car payments, working long hours loaded down by too much stress. Under these conditions it's easy to become a shell, a hollow emotionally repressed automaton walking on some sort of cultural treadmill believing I'm actually getting ahead. When life becomes this, then discussion about the importance of the journey becomes all but lost. Discussion about God, about what he's doing becomes reduced to the Sunday drive home after church. A sermon evaluation, sometimes positive and sometimes negative, becomes a part of the training of the future generation. The evaluation gets mixed in with complaints about the church's troubling trajectory, mixed in with some complaints about the people I saw who happen to disturb me. All this is usually followed by a mechanical prayer for lunch, and then later on, an equally mechanical bedtime prayer. Faith becomes mundane, and I set this example for my family, then I wonder why my kids don't want to go to church. At this point, is there a difference between what I'm doing and students tossing around a meaningless cultural expression which neutralizes the power of God's name? Not really. Not in the sense neither person involved understands their importance in God's kingdom.

By God's grace, I also know another path exists for parents to walk down. A path exists where we can't be self-absorbed, where in order to walk it, we have to meet Christ daily and lay our burdens and sins at the cross. I must be willing to meet Christ and express my own inadequacies and my own shortcomings in connecting to purpose and meaning. At this place, I'm able to look outside of myself and see my importance to Christ and to what he is doing. Here, when I pray for the food, I thank God for providing our family with provisions and a shelter for I realize that my own efforts may provide a structure, but that structure is nothing without spiritual food and living water. And when I kneel at the side of my children's beds at the end of the day to pray for them, I pray God will not only protect their lives but also allow them to live lives of purpose and meaning, regardless of task. I express the importance of praying for wisdom, and we talk about the necessity of loving those around us, especially those who we don't want to like or love. We talk about looking for the kids at school who may not have a friend and then looking for opportunity to be a friend to that person, and we talk about the language that comes from our mouths, how it is connected to what is on our hearts. We speak of healing and forgiveness. And in our conversation we speak about God as a central reference.

On the surface, the difference between the two approaches is minute—one I serve God and the other I pay lip service to God. The outcome though is ground shaking. On the one side I'm disconnected from myself, from my family and from my friends. On the other side though, I experience life and I'm able to share that life with all those around me, especially my children and students.

CHAPTER 12

The Return to Raw Faith

Right after I graduated from university a good friend and I took a road trip to Alaska. One of the most memorable parts of the trip happened well before we witnessed the Alaskan grizzlies ripping apart salmon flesh close enough to hear the tearing and proved to be more impressive than the mountains we climbed or the fish we caught. In Northern British Columbia, we took a left off the dirt road we'd been traveling for hours on already, and we headed west for another 120 kilometers on another gravel road. I was interested in the area because my grandfather lived the life of a prospector around these parts, and he spent many years searching for riches specifically around a village called Telegraph Creek, population, just over three hundred. I decided that I wanted to take the long drive in to the area where he, according to family legend, discovered the largest copper deposit in North America. A sign stood at the entrance to the long gravel road stating that any vehicle traveling this road must be able to negotiate 20 percent grades. I had no idea whether or not my two-wheel-drive vehicle could handle the steep hills, but as far as my twenty-three-year-old brain could compute, the only way to find out was to actually travel the road. The gravel road took us through some of the most beautiful country I've ever experienced. We drove beside and through what is known as the Grand Canyon of the Stikine. As we left a plateau and descended down one of the 20 percent hills toward the canyon floor, we happened upon two blond grizzly bears who both stood up on their hind legs as we drove closer. I fumbled for my Nikon, but the camera-shy pair returned to all fours and ran off the road before I could snap the shot.

When we finally arrived in the village, we saw nothing but a few houses and an old church. Being a Saturday, we decided we'd see what time the service started the following day and then make sure we packed up camp the following morning so as to be on time for the service. The next morning we packed up our camping gear and headed off toward the classic styled frontier church. The white building with windows spaced evenly all the way down the side was built in the shape of a box with a steep pitched roof and a steeple rising skyward. Nathan and I arrived about ten minutes early and were surprised to be the first. We tried the doors but they were locked. We waited about twenty minutes before we began to realize that maybe the building was nothing more than an historic site. As we were walking back to our car to leave, a large rusty Suburban roared up beside us. Two people jumped out and apologized for being late. The husband and wife introduced themselves and informed us they were filling in while the pastor took holidays. They unlocked the doors, and we walked into the cold building. Like the outside, the interior had never been updated, and the wood floors creaked as we carefully selected our wooden pew.

Four people attended church in Telegraph Creek that day. My traveling companion, Nathan, and I doubled Sunday morning attendance. I can't remember the couple's names, but the lady started the service by pulling out her guitar and leading worship. She led from the front and sang loudly, and her voice echoed off the wooden surroundings as we joined in singing praises together. The songs seemed to warm the building. After three or four songs, she placed her instrument back in the case and sat down. Her husband pulled himself from his pew and walked up to the pulpit. He appeared noticeably nervous as he steadied himself with the lectern and looked down for an uncomfortable period of time. When he gathered his nerves, he looked up and began to speak, then interrupted himself and said that he should start with prayer. He did, and then he launched into his five-minute sermon. I wish I could remember what he talked about, but all I remember is an illustration he used about Mother Theresa's work, so he may have preached on sacrifice and service. Regardless, when he finished, he prayed again, and then he went and sat back down beside his wife, obviously relieved.

The planned service couldn't have lasted more than twenty minutes, but when I look back I realize that the service continued after the sermon. The couple came over and sat in the pew in front of us and began to converse. We reintroduced ourselves and then thanked them for leading. They inquired about what brought us to their small church, and we ended up talking for over an hour about Christ, about our testimonies, about our journey, and about life.

Raw Faith

This particular morning at an old church in the middle of nowhere, the setting and the people so far removed from university debates and tawdry urban church services, reminded me that my faith core does not reside in issues that involve faith. The center of my faith did not depend on my education, my strengths, or my ability to debate the hot topics of the day. This may sound ridiculously simplistic, but sitting and speaking with these people brought me to a place where I realized Christ alone exists at the core of my faith. We had Christ alone in common, and that proved enough. The message and the music, the well-worn and hard pews, the cold building, the length of the service—all seemed to stop short of what a powerful, life-altering service should be. But that morning in a building beside the Stikine River in northern British Columbia, God's presence rested on us.

I know that discussing the essence of the faith is a risky issue because if you ask three different Christians what the core of the Christian faith is, you'll potentially get nine different answers. But raw faith, a faith that depends on Christ alone, requires me to love God with my entire being as an act of worship, asks me to daily deny self so that I may first serve Christ and others in order that his message may live through my life and infiltrate other's lives. Raw faith fosters a desire for redemption, forgiveness, prayer, Scripture reading, and obedience to God's Word.

I'm not saying that we should not worry about false prophets and messages that lead congregations astray because that can happen and we need to be on our guard. And I never think we should neglect the "iron-sharpening-iron" type of discussions that happen between believers, but we need to restore balance. Right now the debates and the chasing after fads are the portly boy on the teeter-totter that won't let us down. The scales have been tilted to one side for so long that we constantly neglect bringing ourselves as offerings to Christ. As we provide our lives as offerings, God's presence engages with our humble hearts.

I don't reduce in order to take away from the mysteries of the faith, nor to say that any individual can only ever be involved in anything but raw faith. My purpose is simply to serve as a reminder that raw faith should be every Christians' primary motivation, regardless of whatever cultural battle or trend they find themselves engaged in. In saying this, I'm fully aware Christ calls some to stand up and fight against theories, philosophes, and laws contrary to the Scriptures. But in these battles, one must never neglect the reason behind why they fight. An individual detached from the core, from the very reason why they stand up and fight, is the same person who becomes concerned about nothing else other than self and winning spiritual arguments. They become the pastor who's lost all connection, to the congregation and to God; the theology professor at the Christian university who's more interested in theory than God; and the Christian-school teacher who cares more about content than souls. When we forget about the core, we naturally default to religious ceremony and tradition rather than relationship with the Savior. When we neglect raw faith, we transform into pew occupants rather than eternal residents.

We must grapple with cultural waves and scientific theories that contradict scriptural truths. We need to offer an answer to those who ask, to those who want to engage. Take the Creation versus evolution debate. Universities educate some of Christianity's greatest minds in order to stay current in this debate. Intelligent individuals earn doctorates in this area and dedicate their entire lives to defending biblical accounts of humanity's origins. This is good, but we have to be careful that Christianity never equals the Creation debate. That Christianity does not become the pro-life versus pro-choice debate. The faith offers far more. These debates are part of standing up for what is right and good and true, but a day will come where the fight will move to a different topic, and even in my lifetime, we may see the day where our children hear very little about these topics and may even look at us funny when we say that back in the day we debated such issues. The point is that new issues will come and take the place of existing topics, so we have to raise children who understand raw faith—who know what their faith is at its very essence when everything else is stripped away, so they know with their souls that truth resides in God, and God is love. Therefore, no debate is ultimately about winning and losing. Every debate simply directs people toward truth and love, reconciliation and peace. Raw faith starts and ends with Christ. All is secondary to Christ and his redemptive power on a life. Often we have a problem with an idea or a concept being labeled as secondary. If the idea is not primary, then we feel as though it loses validity. How do we dedicate our lives to fighting against a secondary concept? The concepts are only secondary though in reference to our starting point. Because God put an issue on your heart, that issue may be the most important issue in the world to you. Similarly, during a heavy snowfall the road out in front of your house is the most important road. Why does it seem that it takes so long for city snowplows to come and clean this street? Probably because it is a secondary residential road. The road crews will always start with the primary roads and the emergency roads to make sure those remain clear. Labeling a road as secondary does not make it any less of a road. It simply reminds an individual that other roads, affecting an entire community, will be tended to first. In the same way, we should always recognize the primary aspects of faith, and our primary is Christ. Let us tend to the secondary roads that God has called us to only after we've taken care of the primary road.

For as long as I've heard the story from John 8 about the woman the Pharisees brought before Christ, the narrative fascinated me. In the previous chapter the Pharisees send temple guards to remove Jesus as he teaches the crowds gathered around him. When the guards come back without a prisoner, the Jewish leaders question them and the guards respond by saying they had never heard anyone teach the way Jesus does. Though they want him arrested they do not lay a hand on him. When the Pharisees realize the conventional way of sending out the brute squad to bring Christ in does not work, they devise another plan. They try to trap Jesus by drawing him in to their most familiar territory, the law. They exemplify a group who's turned a secondary into a primary. The New Testament presents the Pharisees as a religious group who focuses on the law to the point where they've lost sight of their original target, which is God.

The Pharisees bring a woman caught in adultery before Christ so that he can condemn her. They try to engage the Messiah in their world of rules and laws. They want Jesus to understand that what he teaches falls short, that it is not enough. His teachings are not only blasphemous, according to them, but they are grossly inadequate. Their law answers the "what if" questions. So they bring a "what if" before Christ in the form of a woman caught in the act of sexual indiscretion. In an inhumane act, the Pharisees drag the woman into the arena of public humiliation in order to accomplish their goal of trapping Jesus so they can accuse him.

The Jewish leaders say that the Law requires them to stone her. Two problems exist with this statement. One, their Law did not prescribe a method of execution with the exception of a betrothed virgin caught in adultery, and in that case, both parties needed to be stoned to death. In this particular situation though, Pharisees only present the woman. So they may have been testing Christ on multiple levels, thus, endeavoring to destroy Christ's reputation publicly by proving he did not know the Law as well as they did. On a second level, the Jewish leaders strive to present Jesus with a "lose, lose" scenario. Though their Law required this woman's death, the ruling Romans did not allow the Jews to carry out death sentences. If Jesus gave the go ahead for the execution, he would have found himself in conflict with Roman law. However, Jesus saying no to the leaders' request would mean he was not in support of Jewish Law—the perfect trap.

Jesus's response extends beyond the words coming out of his mouth. First, he avoids engaging in their urgency. He looks down and begins to "write on the ground with His finger" (John 8:6 NIV). For the longest time, I used to wonder what he wrote. I told some friends once that would be one of the first questions I'd ask during the question and answer time in heaven (though I don't actually think there will be one). If there was, I wonder if Jesus would take questions press conference style. Yes, the reporter from *The Daily*, what's your question? Um ... Jesus what did you write on the ground with your finger when the Jewish leaders brought the woman caught in adultery before you as a trap? I wonder if Jesus would respond by saying it's not what he wrote that he wanted to communicate. The action and not the words was the intent of that particular message to the leaders. His actions communicate he would not be drawn into their panic, and he'd rather not be drawn into their secondary issue when a truly pressing issue presented itself. He chooses to avoid their eyes, meaning he chooses to avoid creating a larger problem than they've already created here by publicly disgracing this woman for their own selfish gain. By writing on the ground with his finger, he's saying that your intention is to destroy me, and this woman is collateral damage, but wait for it and ask again and you will see that, not only will I redeem this mess you've created, I'll also lovingly remind everyone present the Law is not the primary issue. God's love is. God's justice, mercy, and grace are more powerful than the Law. Wait for it. Then he stands up and responds, "If any one of you is without sin, let him be the first to throw a stone at her" (John 8:7 NIV). Knowing how many people present could meet this demand, he stoops back down and continues to write on the ground. He continues to communicate without saying a word. Perhaps he knows those who stood in judgment, once they've examined themselves, would find they are unqualified to cast stones, and he knows he is the only one qualified under those conditions to toss the stone.

I erroneously used to think that this narrative was about the woman. Though she only has one line of dialogue, she's central. But she's not the main character. Christ is the protagonist. The nameless woman is prominent in the narrative, but with one statement Christ enables all present to identify with her position. Her redemption not only saves her life, Christ reminds her accusers that any one of them could take center stage when it comes to sin. Christ then sends them away, but he also draws them closer together through the recognition that their own human nature attracts them toward sin and corruption. The Law, that which was designed to keep them from their own demise, now meets its fulfillment in Christ. In this narrative Christ is the center—this is the essence of raw faith.

When he stands up, he reminds us he never redeems us so that we can carry on in our own selfish desires and sinful ways.

He purposes for us to live a life aware of the sin that ensnares us. More than awareness, he desires we rely on him for strength so we are never drawn back into the same trap. The same self-inflicted pressure pulling us down also destroys us and keeps us from existing in his presence. When Christ stands up, he says, "Woman, where are they? Has no one condemned you?" (John 8:10 NIV). She replies, "No one, sir" (John 8:11 NIV). To which he speaks the life-filled words, "Then neither do I condemn you … Go and leave your life of sin" (John 8:11 NIV). Here is your freedom now go and be responsible with it. He says the same to us. Here is your freedom—you no longer have to live under the weight of your sin—now go and be responsible with your new freedom. Here is true life, free from all the traps of sin. Now go and use your freedom for my glory. You are not saved to serve self. You are saved to deny self and follow me.

Raw faith starts with Christ and flows through the individual. This faith works through the individual and then travels outward toward friends, family, and community (church or otherwise). Conversely, superficial faith originates with the culture around us. We take part in trends because we desire more than anything to be part of a group and part of what's happening around us. The problem with culture directed faith is that we, at some point, figuratively end up standing in the crowd with a stone in our hands ready to toss it at the person, or group of people whom we deem a threat to our group's way of life. The antithesis to this way of living, and the path our children should be encouraged to walk along, is one where all originates with the one who sets us free from everything holding us captive, whether it is others or ourselves. Raw faith draws us to the point of redemption each and every day and recalibrates our thoughts and desires. At Christ's side we're reminded that our physical lives are finite and that our selfishness is seemingly infinite. We're reminded that true freedom comes from enslaving ourselves to Christ.

So maybe it's time to recalibrate. When we begin to recognize the penetrating and widespread influence of our quest for personal freedom, we can begin to evaluate where we've lost a balance, where our faith gravitated toward self-improvement rather than a building of the Christian community. In our subconscious quest for personal freedom, we've lost our way and forgotten the importance of the balance that's needed; we've neglected our responsibility and our duty to deny self in order to truly develop a love for Christ and for others. We've forgotten that praise and worship is not confined to Sunday morning, but our lives are to be lived as a sacrifice of praise to God. Our worship becomes a life of denying self, and true freedom exists as a byproduct of the Holy Spirit in our lives giving us the strength to deny self.

And it's not just our generation that gets caught up in trends and popular arguments, whether that trend be engaging mentally so we can avoid taking Christ's message to culture; other generations follow other trends. The most recent generation, those following up behind Generation X have figured out that "hunker down and protect faith" misses the mark. Generally, they now engage culture, going on short-term mission trips, involving themselves in relief organizations. They possess a developed environmental awareness, but this generation too must take care not to engage in these practices for the wrong reasons. We can get caught up in any cause for the wrong reason. We can involve ourselves out of peer pressure simply because others take part. We can perform, can go on a mission trip to discover ourselves, and we can sit in a coffee shop and discuss faith topics because it's trendy to do so. But if we do these activities for selfish gain, we end up at the same place, just a different location. We still end up missing the essence of the issue. The nature of a trend is to be replaced by another. Then what? Do we simply hold on to the dying trend, or do we jump on to the next trend wagon? Christ provides us with a better way. Raw faith transcends trends.

CHAPTER 13

Raw Faith and the Individual: Life beyond Personality

Last night I watched a Ted Talk titled "Are Athletes Really Getting Faster, Better, Stronger" by David Epstein, author of *The Sports Gene.*[22] He initially discussed concepts people generally assume to be true. He stated that had the 1936 hundred-meter record holder, Jesse Owens, been able to time travel and compete in 2013 against Usain Bolt's record-setting time, Owens would have lost by almost 14 feet—a great distance in sprinting terms. Epstein goes on to show a number of examples of new world records in long distance running and swimming, so on the surface a person's left to assume that the athlete is becoming more fine-tuned as the years progress. Then he takes his discussion to a deeper level as he implies this assumption may be too simple.

Epstein goes on to make a case for the advancements in technology being the primary contributing factor to new athletic world records. He discusses the time-traveling Owens again and says that to put the world records side by side, yes one man is faster than the other, but then he goes on to say that had Owens been able to run on the same synthetic track instead of the cinder track that he ran on, had Owens had the same starting blocks as Bolt in 2013 as opposed to his own dug out foot positions, Owens

141

would have not finished the 2013 race 14 feet behind Bolt, but a mere one step behind.

Epstein, if nothing else, uncovers an essential concept when looking at the improvements made to sport over the years. His main point being that people are not necessarily getting faster so much as technology and understanding is improving. In the same way, with an explosion in current brain research, and with all the new theories in reference to personality and the human condition, we may make the assumption that as humans we're becoming better, smarter and more self-aware. Though superficially this appears to be true, the issue of human self-improvement is far more complicated than brain research and personality tests. Undoubtedly, we know more about human biology and psychology than at any point in history, which aids us greatly in moving forward with certain conditions and ailments, but in order to experience peace and ultimate fulfillment an individual has to connect to a level beyond the brain and personality.

Back in the '90s, my psychology professors guided me while we peered deeply into the human condition. We studied theories proposed by Freud, Maslow, and Jung. We debated whether or not a person is born tabula rasa and society made an individual good or evil, and we learned to defend our position on the nature versus nurture debate. Professors walked classes though developmental courses. Even after university, I couldn't seem to escape the exploration of the self. At a church small group my wife and I took a new personality test. This multiple-choice test actually had cool animal names for each personality type. After the test, our group found that we contained all types: lions, golden retrievers, otters, and beavers. We learned that each personality type has traits that can be positive and negative. For example, and I don't know why it's always easiest to pick on the Lion, but this person likes authority, and as a result, they have to be careful not to be too direct or demanding. The lion takes charge but may also get pushy. During the test, I sat beside my wife as she quickly and confidently answered each question, so she finished first or second in the group. The Lions always seem to get through first, with their "let's get this done" mentality. Me on the other hand, I waffled on questions and even asked my wife to help with the question "Do I struggle with decision-making?" when I couldn't seem to decide whether or not I did. Apparently I was not a lion.

Now, years later, personality tests are far more complex. The most popular one I found online, simply called "16 Personalities: Get to know yourself," still maintained an inner core of four personality types, but then has four subcategories that attach themselves to Sentinels, Explorers, Diplomats and Analysts. At first the subcategories are dizzying, identified only by initials as headings. The test though is easy and thorough and not only takes a person to an in-depth description of their personality, but also informs them as to the best career paths to take, the strengths and weaknesses associated with the personality type, and discusses the most suitable matching romantic personality type.

Psychologists discovered much since the origins of personality study. Since the eighteenth century, forward advancement has been made in this field. Initial understanding focused on the exterior. Phrenologists believed that one could understand a person's personality through the measurement of the human skull, and physiognomy was the study of a person's personality based on their appearance. As early as the 1920s, the armed forces used personality tests aid in personnel selection. In the 1950s researchers tried to establish a connection between physical health and personality. The infamous Type A and Type B personalities come from this study. In this study researchers established that the Type A personality, the high stress person who is rigid and ambitious, who is always trying to push themselves and those around them, are more prone to health issues like heart disease and cancer. Though this study took place over four decades, ending in the '90s, I still hear people use this terminology today.

I've heard coworkers say something like watch out for John, he's Type A. Don't get in his way when he's trying to meet a deadline.

In 2012, new information apparently revealed that the tobacco industry funded this research. Interesting. Why would the tobacco industry be so concerned about personalities? When medical research started to point the finger at the tobacco industry as the main cause for heart disease and in an effort to deflect responsibility, the industry began to construct a case that personality, not an intake of smoke into the body, caused ultimate heart failure. The Type A personality is always stressed out. They try to take control of every situation and in doing so create pressure and stress on themselves, and this, not cigarettes (not a multibillion dollar industry), is responsible for heart failure. Provide a solution for the stressed out personality, and we'll find the cure for heart attacks. Have a cigarette Type A individual— that will clear your mind and help to calm you down.

It can be difficult at times not to be cynical when you hear how science and studies can be manipulated and twisted to suit the purpose of an individual or an industry. It happens often, whether on issues like global warming or fish farming, that science can become a tool to protect self-interests. Regardless, the personality study appears to explore deep within an individual, but fails to understand an individual's core. One might assume that the closer civilizations situate themselves to self-enlightenment and self-discovery, the closer an individual comes to self-diagnosis and self-repair. Personality types allow one to relate, but they do not allow one to restore. They allow a person to go, "Hey, that's me. That's the way I react under these circumstances. These are the situations where I'm able to use my skills. This personality type best suits my personality type when searching for a spouse." But what they do not account for is the fact that sometimes a person acts out of character. Sometimes, situations happen to us that we have no control over. Labeling a personality may give a person an indication of how they might respond on the surface, but they do not delve deep beyond the subsurface to the place where guilt resides, the place where the memories repressed since childhood or young adulthood exist. The personality mainly operates from the inside out and deals with our preferences and responses, with our traits and characteristics, but what it does not account for is human nature. Why does a person or an industry sponsor a scientific study simply to propagate biased information when that information is potentially destructive to humans or environments? Why, in some situations, does a person lie to cover their tracks and tell the truth in other situations? Why is it, regardless of personality type, most men struggle with lust? And regardless of personality type, why is it that we all act rashly when angered. Why, personality aside, do we gossip and cut down a fellow human? Why do most women constantly fight against their own insecurities? A deeper level exists within humanity, like an underground water source.

Christ starts with the core. God created variety in personality, but our deepest level, the underground well, is the soul and this is where Christ begins the work of redemption. He starts at the core and begins a work of restoration, so that, regardless of personality, a person may truly live a life of grace, free from the constraints of selfish desires.

Unrestrained self-freedom, on the other hand, leads directly down the path of selfish desire. Selfish desires lead to pleasure escape which eventually intensifies to the point where the receptors for personal pleasure become completely deadened and unable to receive feeling at which case a person can move on to discover a new pleasure escape if they are not completely destroyed by their initial escape. At this point, a person's freedom becomes their captivity. This person who lived a life of freedom, unfettered by religion, or moral boundaries, is now a slave to that which provided the façade of freedom only to eventually entice them down destruction's path.

Then the person who lived a life of restraint and discipline becomes the person who experiences freedom and the person who lived a life desiring nothing more than to please their own desires, switch places. A person who desires ultimate freedom from moral constraint, ends up completely controlled by their own selfish desire and the person who leads a life of discipline is not mastered by his desires. Both can potentially end up in the same place though if the disciplined person becomes a slave to discipline instead of Christ. Discipline becomes his or her god, and this individual walks down a path of judgment leading toward isolation. Christ does not redeem our core, our souls, so that we can then walk upright alone. Raw faith starts with the connection between the self and Christ, but the relationship is not exclusive in nature, like two teenagers in love completely oblivious to all around them.

Christ Reaches Out to Restore the Individual

I wonder if at some point before the Jewish leaders ultimately boiled over and put Christ on trial, they talked about not saying anything at all, because everything they said Christ used as momentum to teach the people crowded around him. I like to think they tried to not say anything, but there were a few of them who just could not hold their tongues. When they rolled their eyes and muttered under their breath, I bet the lead Pharisee in the group gave them the "shut up" look. Don't speak or he'll start teaching again. There were even times where they did not even have to say anything. They just thought it, and Jesus responded to them. Their thoughts weren't even safe. In their morning meeting before they headed out, I envision their leader saying, "Okay, you guys don't say anything. Don't challenge him. Don't even think a thought that challenges him. We've tried this tactic before and it does not work. Don't mentally engage in what he's saying.

He will take your thoughts and your spoken challenges and use them to teach the people, and that is what we really don't want. Just listen to what he's saying and see if we can use his words to secure a conviction. Do this until we can figure out a strategy to deal with this problem." Then right after the meeting they head out to see what Jesus is talking about today, and he's not talking about anything. He's just hanging out with losers: sinners and tax collectors. A rookie Pharisee, I'll call him Thaddeus, leans over to his buddy, and under his breath says, "Why are we so worried about this guy? Look at the lowlifes he's hanging out with." Before he can even snicker at his own statement, Jesus turns and his gaze looks through Thaddeus's eyes right to the depths of his being, and Christ begins to teach. Thaddeus's fellow Pharisees stare at him with a look of disbelief and shake their heads.

Jesus wants to emphasize his point today because raw faith has everything to do with salvation and redemption, so he speaks about the lost, the "sinners," by way of parable, but he really wants to clearly relate this message, so he uses three parables to teach those present about what exactly God is willing to do to redeem an individual's core, regardless of how much their travels have destroyed their souls. Christ starts out with a shepherding analogy. He teaches the group about a shepherd who has a hundred sheep and loses one of them. The shepherd goes out and searches until he brings the lost sheep back to the herd. On the surface the message is of love and redemption, but at another level, Christ reminds the Pharisees that though they think they are better than the lost, the sinners, in God's eyes they are originally part of the same herd and his desire is to restore them to a point of safety under the watchful eye of the shepherd. He's saying, "Hey, Thaddeus, even though you have your group and you feel safe because of your group, which has rules, and abuses those rules to elevate yourselves and put down others, I'm trying to help you see that in my eyes you are all part of the same group and my desire is to restore all of you, whether you think you have it all together and look down on the sinner or you are the sinner."

Just in case you don't get the animal analogy, just in case you consider yourself too good to be compared to an animal, here is another parable for you. It's about money, but it makes the exact same point. If a woman has ten silver coins but loses one, does she not bother with the one she lost? No, of course not. She does everything she can to find that lost coin, even if it's at night and she needs to light lamps and meticulously search all over the house until she finds it. When she finds it, Thaddeus, does she not rejoice with her neighbors? In the same way, when God restores a person's soul, when that person finds their way back to God, there is much rejoicing in heaven, because this "sinner" before you labeled him a "sinner" is an image bearer of God and in need of redemption.

Still sneering, Thaddeus? Is it because I used a woman in the parable? Here is one more for you then. Listen closely, because this one is sure to touch your soul. "There was a man who had two sons …" (Luke 15:11 NIV). At this, Thaddeus feels a lump in his throat even before Jesus proceeds with the rest of the story. One son requests his inheritance early from his father and then heads out and squanders his father's wealth on all that brings dishonor to his family. He spends his money on loose living, on prostitutes, on drinking, on friends, and they are plentiful while he's throwing around his wealth. He lives life to the fullest, unconstrained by all the house rules he grew up with. He throws off the teachings of his father and now truly experiences life—or so he thought. When the son burns through his inheritance, life takes a strange turn for him. His friends leave, and he ends up realizing that he must find work to survive. At this section of the story, Thaddeus tries to deflect the emotions welling up from deep within him. He reverts back to a childish behavior he used to do in school when he felt uncomfortable, so he jabs his friend, contorts his face in a ridiculous manner, sticks out his tongue, rolls his eyes, and shakes his head as if to say, "No wonder this guy hangs out with losers;

he himself is a loser." Deep down, past his ego and his defense mechanisms, the third parable hits him hard, and he knows it. Christ is looking right at him and telling the story of his family. His brother, who he loves dearly, who he protected all through school, who he shielded from the Romans time and time again, he left and wanted nothing to do with God, nothing to do with his family. He looks for him every day but has not been able to locate him—he doesn't know whether or not his little brother is alive or dead. As Jesus continues to speak, the lump gets bigger and eventually makes its way out the corner of his eye and down his cheek.

Jesus goes on to discuss the wayward son in the pig mire, consuming the same food the filthy animals eat, wanting to go home but feeling he's not worthy because of all the atrocities he's committed and because of all the shame he's brought to his family. At this point, Thaddeus's mouth moves without thought or control and he utters, "Come home, brother. Please come home." The Pharisees standing around him shoot him disapproving glances, but Thaddeus is unaware because he's captured by the Teacher's eyes. He now listens intently as the younger brother makes his way home, and the father is there waiting, overpowered by emotion when he sees his son limping along the road taking him closer the place where he belongs. They sprint to each other and embrace. The lost made his way home.

Christ goes farther with this parable though, past the rejoicing where the other two ended. He discussed an older brother, and the older brother is so overcome by a sense of injustice he does not care his kid brother is home. He goes straight to his father and complains about fairness. "Why is it that I didn't get this treatment? Don't I deserve special treatment?" he says. Thaddeus recognizes where the Teacher is heading and he wants nothing to do with judgment anymore. All he knows is that when he showed up and labeled those surrounding Jesus as losers, he placed the same label on his brother. He's ashamed of his words. This realization breaks his heart to the point that his soul is exposed and he determines he will seek Jesus out later and beg of him to help he and his brother come home. He knows that when the others find out, he'll be considered a traitor, an apostate, a loser, but he's never felt more peace. He's never felt more at home. Jesus smiles. Heaven rejoices.

Father God values the loser because we are all his children. Sometimes, he searches for us and sometimes he allows us to search for him. He desires to restore relationship with his children, but the restoration process does not stop with the individual.

What Identity Is Their Inheritance?

What will we pass along to our teens? An attitude of judgment or a discerning heart filled with grace. We want nothing more than to fill them with knowledge, to teach the morals presented in the Bible. We want them to internalize these and make them their own, so they can go on to live a life controlled by nothing other than their savior. I've spent the better portion of my working career teaching the Bible to high school students, and I recognize the importance of teaching in an engaging way, and helping the next generation understand the basic principles of their faith. This we must never give up on. We teach the Scriptures whenever the opportunity presents itself and we teach the Scriptures even when the opportunity does not present itself. But how do we load our students, our children with biblical knowledge without creating modern-day Pharisees and older prodigal brothers? How do we pass along information without implying that knowledge is more important than other ways to love our God? How do we balance knowledge of him and grace for others?

The beginning of the answer starts with one simple recognition—we are not saved so that we can selfishly hoard Christ's riches. As people of faith in our culture, we project a subconscious propensity to act in this manner. I'm responsible for my own faith walk and you're responsible for yours. However, each parable in Luke 15 does not end with the lost being found. Each parable expands to include others: the angels, the neighbors, and the older brother. In this way these parables connect to the parable in Luke 10 and create a much-needed reminder—that when Christ redeems our souls he requires that we not allow the restoration to be self-serving. Another answer to the riddle may also come from a different encounter Jesus has with an expert in the law. In Luke 10, the teacher asks Christ what he must do to inherit eternity. Christ asks him a question in response but does so in a way that allows the teacher to comfortably respond. He asks the teacher about his field of expertise—Christ asks him what the law says and the teacher, according to Christ, responds correctly. The teacher replies, "Love the Lord your God with all your heart and with all your soul and with all your strength and with all your mind … and love your neighbor as yourself" (Luke 10:27 NIV). The teacher though wants more from Christ because the answer is too simple—he knows this already, so he asks Christ a second question, and here is where the true teaching takes place, the teaching beyond the law by the mind that came to fulfill the law. The teacher says, "And who is my neighbor?" (Luke 10:29 NIV). To which Jesus must have rubbed his hands together in delight and thought, *I was hoping you'd ask.*

Christ instructs the teacher using a parable. He goes on to tell a didactic story about a man traveling along a road and running into robbers who stole everything, beat him, and left him half dead on the side of the road. The way is well traveled, and three people come along. A priest first saw the wounded man, but he carries on. He's got much to do, large responsibilities to tend to, and may even become unclean by helping the injured man. As a side note, some translations even say that the beaten traveler was Jewish, same as the priest, and the second man who avoided the injured man, the Levite. He also would have been in a hurry and had much to tend to in the temple, so he passed by on the other side of the road.

It's the third traveler who stops and helps out the dying man. The other two probably thought someone less busy would come along and help this guy out. In this story that someone was not a teacher of the law or another priest, that someone was a Samaritan. The history between Jews and Samaritans was not a good one. One could go so far as to say they were enemies who wanted nothing to do with one another. But in Christ's parable it's the person who had every reason not to stop and help, who actually tends to him on the side of the road and then places him on his donkey and takes him to a place where the injured man can heal from his wounds. The Samaritan then goes beyond all expectations and pays his lodging and tells the hotel attendant he'll be back to take care of the rest of the account.

Did the Samaritan stop because he had nothing urgent to do? No. In this way, he identifies with the priest and the Levite. He brings him to the hotel and can't stay, but says he'll return to settle the payment. Christ says much about the restoration of the soul in the parable, and really this is what the parable is all about. Remember the original question—what must I do to inherit eternal life? And really Christ's comments about the soul here, lead one to answer the most difficult riddle presented to us when it comes to teaching our teens much and not having them simply absorb like sponges but also be squeezed providing water to a thirsty generation. Christ says that our neighbor is not someone who we simply love; our neighbor is also someone who we hate, who we despise. Christ starts with love, not with the self. When Christ restores our souls, he asks us to start with love (which then by very nature must be a selfless act) and not necessarily how we feel about an individual. When Christ restores the soul, he gives us strength to look past the exterior or the physical (race, body shape, gender, sexual orientation), past the personality (lion, beaver, otter, golden retriever) and enables us to see what he sees:

a soul in need of redemption. So even if a person is an enemy, for whatever reason, this same person has a soul in need of healing. In an interesting point of similarity, Christ's final instructions to the teacher of the law resemble those he speaks to the woman caught in adultery: "Go and ..." Christ says to the teacher of the law, "Go and do likewise," (Luke 10:37 NIV) and to the adulterous woman, "Go now and leave your life of sin" (John 8:11 NIV). When we've experience enlightenment or forgiveness in a certain area, it's not intended to stop there. We're to "Go ..." Our newfound freedom also becomes a newfound responsibility. We've grown accustomed to spending our spiritual wealth on ourselves, and our children see this. Our soul's restoration is not only intended to heal the entire self, but is also intended to provide an avenue along which others can find healing. Those others may not even be someone that we're comfortable with or have anything in common with. They may be someone who's wronged us in unpardonable ways in the past. Christ at work in us means we naturally desire to reach out to other fractured souls.

The apostle Paul recognizes this as well. He says in his second letter to the Corinthians, that "If anyone is in Christ, he is a new creation: the old has gone and the new has come!" (2 Corinthians 5:17 NIV). We often stop there because we like the idea that we're reborn, but Paul does not say that we're reborn merely for the purpose of a restored self. A few sentences later he says that in this "ministry of reconciliation" to Christ we are His "ambassadors, as though God were making his appeal through us" (2 Corinthians 5:20 NIV). Now that we're saved, we can carry his message to others. This then could very well be the solution to the riddle, the answer to why the Christian faith loses a large number of teens after they leave high school. What if intellectual skepticism is the façade, just the smoke needing to be waded through? Because if we are losing our teens for reason of intellect, maybe it's because we've misled them to believe the greatest commandment is to love the Lord their God with all their minds. If so, we've grossly confused them. According to the greatest commandment our love for God envelops our entire being: body, mind, and soul. And then is accompanied by a second: to love our neighbor as ourselves. If we've merely been loading them with information, and with knowledge, then we've only been doing a good job in one area, and unfortunately, we've been the ones who've tilted the scales against them. Yet in the area of raw faith, we can never simply satisfy one aspect of the self, otherwise we encourage other areas of the self to take control. By simply nursing our children's spiritual intellect, we neglect the rest of the temple. We allow them to believe that it's fine to retain control over other rooms in the temple.

Encouraging our children to seek the fullness of raw faith, this means encouraging them to surrender themselves in their entirety. Christ requires all: our emotions, our thoughts, and our desires. Raw faith then requires one more step, and for those of us who exist in twenty-first-century North America, this step may be the largest step for us to take. We've been conditioned to be saved for the betterment of our own futures. We believe we need to take care of ourselves first. We build our own empires and shrines to celebrate our personal achievements. I am most important. And it is here that raw faith requires us to obliterate a shaky mental construct and then rebuild. The bridge that Christ requires us to rebuild is the one between ourselves and others. As we reach out to those around us, God is not requiring us to be spiritually absent-minded. He's simply requiring us to see the intellect as one component intended to balanced with other key elements.

Maybe this is why we've gone down the road of satisfying the intellect because if we desire to know more and learn more, then we feel like we're doing something for God, but we still get to control other areas of our lives. In pursuit of increasing spiritual IQ we've missed the key truth: if we simply fight on this battleground then we will eventually lose every time. Christ reconciles the mind, but he does so for a purpose. He restores our mind so we can use it for his glory. In this way then, the greatest destroyer of raw faith may not be intellectual skepticism, but a use of the intellect to avoid connecting with others who possess fractured souls. Relationships in this fallen world are sure to be messy and create hurt. People stink and carry sickness. Others are difficult to understand and may not even pay attention to what we have to say, but Christ requires us to love others, even if they've hurt us or we don't have time for them.

One of my good friends, I'll call him Greg, told me a story about why it is he has absolutely no use for the Christian faith. He grew up in a small prairie town where most people are farmers, and most farmers know each other. On one particular Sunday morning, he was out for a walk and in the distance he noticed someone sprawled out in a large mud puddle in a parking lot beside the main road through town. As he got closer, he recognized the person on the ground as the town drunk—he had obviously passed out and fallen into the dirty water. To make matters worse, the time it took for Greg to arrive to aid the fallen man, a number of cars passed by the drunk and simply kept on driving. The drivers were in a hurry, and the three or four that went by all turned into the same parking lot—the one with the building with the large steeple and the cross. They drove by a man in need of help to go to a place where they could learn about reaching out to those in need. I'm sure lots of good reasons exist for why those in their Sunday bests did not have time to stop, and I wonder if any of those reasons ran through the priest's and the Levite's head in Luke 10: I have to help out in Sunday school today, I have to set up communion, or I'm in charge of the sound for the service. Maybe the thoughts were more judgmental in nature: when will he ever learn his lesson, that will teach him for drinking too much, or he's always been a loser.

Greg stooped down and pulled the drunk from the puddle, took him to a store and bought him some dry clothes and then took him for coffee. When Greg told me this story, distain dripped from his lips. He spoke with much hurt in his voice and connects this story to why he has zero time for faith, and even less time for Christians. He can't seem to reconcile the fact that none of these Christians stopped to help. When he told the story, I felt ashamed and could not give him a response. I just sat and listened. But I thought a lot about going back to that moment and responding with something other than an embarrassed silence, and I still don't really know what I would say to him. Christians talk a lot, so maybe it won't be words that change his mind about the faith. Then again, maybe he'll want to discuss it again one day. My response might be different. I may tell him I've been the person who's driven by and I've also been the person who's stopped. Meaning, just like everyone else, a person of faith is not immune to making mistakes. And those people he talks about with such distain, those people who drove right past the drunk that day, Christ teaches us that if one of them fell helplessly into a muddy puddle, that we should never walk past them and think, they had it coming. Christ requires us to go one step farther; he requires us to love our enemy, for our enemy is also our neighbor.

As a side note, the day after I included the above anecdote about Greg, it was a Saturday morning and I had to drive my son to a soccer tournament in another community forty-five minutes away. We had to meet the team at 8:30 a.m. in a store parking lot near the soccer pitch to find out where we were going. On the way out the door my wife asked if I'd place a garage sale sign on the post at the four-way stop near our house. As I left the house, a little frustrated because we were already a few minutes late, I grabbed the sign and headed for the door. I quickly drove down to the intersection and jumped out of the car, ran across the street and hammered up the sign. *Good*, I thought as I ran back across the road, *we can still make it on time.* Then a voice came from the other direction, "Excuse me sir, where are you going? I need a ride to Merecroft Street. Can you give me a ride?" I looked over, and saw a disheveled native lady, struggling to walk in a straight line in my direction, like I'd already said yes to her plea. My initial though was that of the priest and the Levite. I had to get my son to his soccer game; I could not make him late for this important game. Then the words that I wrote the day before, Greg's story and Christ's parable returned to my mind. My neighbor needed a ride, because she was still drunk and disoriented from the night before.

She got into the passenger seat, and we took the five-minute ride to Merecroft Street. I introduced her to my son sitting in the back seat, and she said, "Hello, young man. I'm sorry I stink, but I drank last night, I never made it home, and I don't know where I am right now. All I know is that I have to be at work by 11:00." I told her she still had a few hours before she had to start. Then she went on to talk about other jobs she'd lost and said that she could not lose this one. She spoke of wanting a better future, so we talked about accomplishing dreams and the importance of doing a job to the best of one's ability, and the importance of making the most of every opportunity. She sat and listened. Then I dropped her off at a coffee shop two doors down from her place of employment, and she thanked me for the ride and said she'd just go in and drink coffee until her shift started.

We headed away, me with thoughts about what I was going to do if my son's team had already left the meeting spot, and how was I going to find the field? How was I going to make sure that he got to his soccer game on time if I could not find the field?

Then my son spoke. He did not speak about his excitement for his upcoming game; he spoke in a terribly concerned voice. "Daddy," he said, "She did not sleep in her own bed last night."

"No, son," I replied, "She drank too much, she did not know how to get home, and all her friends left her."

"She must have been scared," my ten-year-old said with a quiver in his voice.

"Yes, maybe she was, but she knows where she is now," I said.

"Daddy, I'm so glad that we were there to help her ... and I never want to drink too much even when I'm older."

I smiled. "That's a wise choice son."

The rest of the drive proved to be the longest teachable moment I've experienced with my youngest to that point in his life. He had many questions, and our encounter that morning put him in a place where he listened intently about the way Jesus turned water into wine, about how the Bible instructs us not to be drunk, about how my father and grandfather both faced lifelong struggles with alcoholism. He listened, he asked questions, he interacted, and though the conversation centered on a heavy topic, we never felt weighed down. We talked, we joked, and we expressed concern. And after all was said and done that morning, we pulled into the parking lot at 8:30—right on time—but that didn't seem to matter as much as the connection we'd made with God, with each other, with a neighbor, on that particular morning.

Raw faith. Christ restores our souls, so that we can be involved in the supernatural next step—sharing with our neighbors. Sometimes, faith is that simple. We want to complicate matters though. We want to ask Christ who our neighbor is, and we want to join in cerebral debates about the tension between faith and works. There is a real danger that exists at the end of this road and the danger is that of busyness and fruitless faith. We engage in conversation, we overthink, and we can take time to do this, but we can't seem to figure out how to find time to show concern or build relationship with our neighbor. In church groups and committees we can create strategic plans with target percentages. From the pulpit, we can preach that we will reach 10 percent of the community by 2016, but sometimes our neighbor's needs fall outside of our targets. Helping out our neighbors might mean that, percentages aside, they might smell of alcohol when you pick them up, they might puke in your new SUV, and they might swear in front of your children.

Generally speaking, right now our faith culture is neat and tidy. We're saved, and the people in our faith community are saved, so we don't need to worry about reaching out to our neighbor. With this thought our faith becomes fractured. We create a sanitized faith culture. Then we wonder why our children fall away from the faith? It could very well be that the faith they've inherited from us is an amputated faith. Raw faith is never intended to stop with the individual. Raw faith restores the individual so that the individual can become an ambassador of healing to the community—from he to me to thee.

CHAPTER 14

Avoiding the Community Pitfalls

We want to continually push our teens past isolation, past the self-absorbed state, toward a fruitful life where they recognize the needs of their neighbors and where they understand that Christ requires us to reach beyond ourselves. The ability to see beyond self is good and right. To listen to our restored souls as they call out to hurting souls is to begin to see the world the way that Christ sees the world. Yet just because it is good and right, just because it is the way Christ intended for us to live does not mean that the road will be easy to travel. We live in a fallen world, so it is necessary to accept that even the right way is lined with obstacles and challenges. We can help others but experience hurt as a result. We can reach out but be rejected. The direction we travel is not easy, yet Christ gives us grace enough for the journey, and in that, we find peace in the midst of turmoil. Our connectedness to Christ results in a sense of purpose through trying circumstances. This said, we isolate and recoil for good reason: though community is safer than isolation, community like the rest of life is not perfect. Community not only has its pitfalls, sometimes more people simply means more catastrophic the disasters.

Any time we involve ourselves with others we are, figuratively speaking, on the same school bus all going in the same direction. It sounds like a great idea. And for the most part there is much benefit to this. We are all on board for the same purpose. So why is there conflict? Why do some individuals get in fights and others sit quietly trying to mind their own business? Why is there disagreement over the seating arrangement and why is it that the cool kids get to sit in the back of the bus and the more nerdy kids sit up near the bus driver? Why do those who are different feel attacked and ostracized? The more questions I ask about riding the school bus, the more I begin to realize that many of these questions apply to faith based institutions as well (except for the back of the bus question possibly). So why, in a place where those gathered desire to honor God, why in a place where hearts are changed, why do we face some of the same problems as a bus full of junior high students?

The simple answer—because as much as we desire Christ, we drift away at times and succumb to our own selfishness and human nature. And we carry that with us when we meet together, so problems have always existed within the community of believers and will continue to exist until the point we transition into eternity.

Conformity: Good from Afar but Far from God

As interesting as it would be to explore all the conceivable problems, I am going to focus on the few that can potentially have the most adverse long-term effects on our teens. The first and possibly the most destructive is the mindless march toward conformity. A chief desire for a community of believers should be unity and not conformity. Unity recognizes the importance of diversity and fosters an atmosphere where members recognize the hazards of mindlessness and egocentricity. A faith-based institution that incubates an atmosphere of unity is comprised of individuals who, not simply tolerate, but appreciate not everyone is like them. A purpose exists for the person who pays attention to every detail and understands the importance of structure and tedious details. On the flip side, a person who sees the need for grace in every situation, beyond the rules and the traditions, who emphasizes love beyond the confining policies, is also very necessary. Not only this but a recognition must be in place where a person matures to the point where they see their own blind spots, and their own shadows, and also accepts others for their strengths and weaknesses. In terms of Paul's analogy in 1 Corinthians 12 the feet can take us places, but they can also stink after a long day of walking in shoes that don't breathe very well. The nose can be a perceptive sense but it can also drip or can get plugged up. The arms can do much work, but they can also ache when overworked or when not used for a long period of time.

To carry on with Paul's analogy, the chapter in its entirety proves to be a deep vein of gold waiting to be mined. He acknowledges the different roles needed in the body of Christ, and he even places them in a certain hierarchy. "God has appointed first of all apostles, second prophets, third teachers, then workers of miracles ..." (1 Corinthians 12:28 NIV). Before Paul discusses a level of importance associated with each role, he appears to define importance. All parts of the body are indispensable, meaning all parts are needed in order for the body to function. So "importance" here must be carefully defined. Importance does not mean an individual who possesses certain gifts is more necessary, importance simply means certain gifts incur more responsibility. Our human nature naturally elevates the people who have more responsibility and who are good at dispensing their gifts. Because we gravitate toward importance, larger numbers of people are often attracted to the pastor rather than the groundskeeper. This then can cause people lacking pastoral gifts to desire a pastoral role, and can cause a person's insecurity to ignore their own gifts, desiring a position that does not match their skill set. When this happens, churches suffer, Christian organizations suffer, and the individual suffers. In reference to individuals in the body of Christ, "God has arranged the parts in the body, every one of them, just as he wanted them to be" (1 Corinthians 12:18 NIV). When the right people are in the right positions using their gifts for God's glory, unity is achievable.

Each part of the body is essential, regardless of levels of responsibility. The units that seem unimportant, "That seem to be weaker are indispensable" (1 Corinthians 12:22 NIV). This is an example of perfect unity. Each part performing the role God designed for it, and no one wishing they were doing a role they do not have the gifts for, and no one looking down on others whose roles may be less glamorous. In such an environment, an individual does not covet another's strengths and avoids exacerbating another's weaknesses. Ideally, this is the picture of the faith community in which we want to raise our teens. For in this environment, the individual is understood and the individual is also not pushed to isolation.

In the faith community, where unity is a core value, teens generally grow into their skills and gifts. They learn to see their abilities as an avenue along which they can glorify their Creator. Their skills do not become a catalyst for accomplishing selfish desires, but a means to experience fulfillment and connect themselves to those around them. Their skills aid others who do not possess that particular skill set, because each person is unique but not unto themselves—each person is unique so that they can fulfill an intricate and essential role. Each teen grows and matures to a point where they recognize their talents, and the people around them value them first because they are a child of God and second because each individual's skill set is crucial. This is healthy and produces and perpetuates a dynamic, multigenerational faith environment. Each part of the body plays a vital role in functioning together as a complete unit. The breath of Christ alone engenders this community.

The flip side to unity is what we must be wary of for our teens. Teens are in a place where they naturally push boundaries. Their world requires them to want to know why a certain rule is the way it is, and they want to know why they have to do something a certain way. Essentially they are infant adults, so they may not have learned to attach social graces to their questioning and to their probing, and they may not have any type of perspective attached to levels of importance or consequence. Though this can be frustrating, a silver lining exists: their push allows for culture to move forward thus providing freshness and rejuvenation. Teens, for the most part, will grow and mature and the social graces will be learned along the way. Some learn through experience and others can learn from siblings and classmates' mistakes. But because teens push in disrespectful ways, and because they do so many things that do not make sense to those in authority, our natural response is to push back and engage in their world of confusion, rather than seeing the situation for what it is and for what it could potentially become and then choosing to steer it in a different direction. As a result, communities that teens are a part of can easily degenerate into a place of conformity. I've seen it in schools I've worked in and churches I've been a part of, where the emphasis becomes unity's opposite. Community actually degenerates into conformity, and conformity could quite possibly be one of the most dangerous pressures that our Christian teens unknowingly face.

Conformity is the unhealthy desire of an organization to have each of its individual members think the same way. It is produced by fear and manifests itself through control and causes individuals to lose their self-identity and take on the identity of the group. So at a time when a person's identity is most vulnerable, in their teens, this is when a person fights the hardest to explore and discover their identity. Conformity undermines an individual's desire to search. When an institution focuses on rules first, and all people who are part of the institution must adhere to a certain set of rules in order to be a part of what's going on, this is a telltale sign an institution has concerning problems needing serious attention. I'm not implying that organizations cannot have rules and regulations—that would be ridiculous. However, concerning problems exist when rules overshadow relationship, spirit, and vision. Every institution whether faith based or not, needs to have rules, regulations and guidelines in order to be effective. For example, the schools I've been a part of have dress codes and codes of conduct in place; some schools even have uniforms and hair policies. Along with schools, all other jobs I've worked at require either uniforms or adherence to a dress code. This is common, so the problem is not the rules. The problem becomes the intent and the balance. Those in authority should have the proper intention for enforcing a rule (the leader requires everyone to wear a turtle neck because he wears one to cover up a scar on his neck—not a good reason; whereas, everyone in the company must wear a collared shirt with a tie because this looks classy and our company wants employees to look sharp when representing our product—good reason).

Balance looks different from intent but is equally important. Institutions have a vision, and rules should be implemented in order to compliment the vision and not the other way around. Vision creates a positive atmosphere and a spirit of unity. Ideally, vision creates a desire from within an individual to want to be part of a group. Rules help to maintain a standard in order to maintain the vision. When vision is skewed or lost and all that remains are outdated rules, this becomes detrimental, to the organization and to the individual. Rules become the primary focus and the individual must be tamed. An atmosphere where the person must be stripped of his or her individuality is a toxic environment. I use the word toxic purposely here. The word *toxic* originates from the Greek and originally meant poison put on the tip of arrows. An organization that lacks forward vision is toxic in its most original form. Rules become like poison arrows, targeting the outer shell and slowly killing an individual's identity. Vision on the other hand, gives people the choice. Do you want to be part of what's going on? You choose. If yes, bring all your passion and creativity with you because this institution can use it. We have guidelines to protect our vision, but if you want to be part of what's going on here, those guidelines may require an adjustment but you will not find them taxing. Organizational vision should create a community where individuals want to come and engage in. This is why schools have spirit days and sporting events and outdoor clubs, because it's essential to create an atmosphere that students are proud to be a part of.

Within church groups, conformity originates when the group falls from the ridge that makes up responsibility and freedom, headlong into the valley of responsibility. In this valley, all Christians must think a certain way and act a certain way. And it's understandable why groups can end up in this place. My guess is that it originates from two different places. One could be fear. Different faith cultures believe differently about how much we should engage with the world. Some completely withdraw while others have assimilated with culture to the point where differentiating them becomes impossible. However, most parents and leaders who care about their children also want to protect them from any harm. We want them to act a certain way so they don't go down the same path we went down and experience the same hurt we experienced. In the short term, the easiest way to accomplish this task this is to impose rules.

Conformity can also be the result of confusion. Leaders can falsely assume that the result of Christlikeness is for Christians to become more like each other. Here we must be careful. I don't think that just because we all desire to be more like Christ we will end up thinking and acting the same way. Christians don't need to all grow their hair the same way (the clean-cut pushed to one side, for example), and we definitely don't need to dress the same way (males in suits and women in dresses to the ankles, for example). This line of thinking is detrimental and can carry even farther than outward appearance to inward beliefs. Some people in Christian circles believe that if you are a Christ follower you will end up becoming very meek and mild-tempered. You will respond politely and without confrontation in every circumstance. In short, you will become like them because they strive to be Christlike, and so should you. This line of thinking goes beyond the individual and can be found in some of Christianity's most immense blunders throughout history. Missionaries who go to different cultures and are unable to differentiate between Christian principles and cultural constructs often end up stripping a culture of their uniqueness and replacing one culture for another. If Christianity is true, then it should be true for every culture, and a person should be able to live in their culture and see Christ work through them, all the while purifying them and purifying their culture. A work of cultural redemption most likely will take multiple generations. In the same way, Christ at work in an individual does not mean their personality will be changed so they will be more like their pastor who is more like Christ. It means their soul and their person will be redeemed, so that they will become more Christlike in their service to God and to the community of believers and the community at large. The work of redemption means Christ restores so an individual may discover purpose in whom Father God created them to be, and they may fulfill their purpose as they relate to others. Is everyone a pastor? Is everyone a mechanic? Is everyone a gardener? Is everyone a doctor? No. Christ does not restore us by placing a cookie-cutter over every individual in a group and then standing back he says, "Oh good, now they all look the same and behave in the same manner." On the contrary, he invites us to be part of what he is doing and he says, "I will restore you so you experience purpose in the work you do for me. And you will notice I have numerous people working with me who have different personalities and skill sets. They are likeminded in the sense that I've rebuilt them and they are all willing to work toward my common vision, but the church functions best when people begin to see the beauty of diversity."

Beauty in diversity? In church? A person may argue that there is no diversity within the moral rules and at the core of the Christian faith, to which I would agree. But back to a vision that creates unity—the core Christ invites us to be a part of does not negate diversity, it nurtures diversity. The core vision says come if you want and be a part of what we're about. Here is a set of moral guidelines that enable you to fully experience a deep relationship with he who designed the organization. The organization has rules, yes, and those rules need to be followed. To that end they are an essential part of what goes on. They are essential, but they are also secondary. The vision, which is comprised of redemption, love, forgiveness, righteousness, grace, peace, and justice, that is essential and primary. Internalize the vision and the rules become a mere extension of the purpose.

Conformity primarily concerns itself with the external. If an individual acts a certain way, then he must therefore believe a certain way. Make someone do the right thing and then they will eventually walk the right path. Right? No more treacherous a road exists than forcing a young adult to constantly walk along this highway. At best, conformity can save a person from making destructive decisions for a period of time, but this depends on the personality of the individual. Some individuals possess personality traits that allow them to function well within these parameters. The more passive individuals can learn to exist within this environment but the strong-willed boundary pushers will more than likely resent this environment and all associated with it.

An atmosphere of conformity is also a breeding ground for deception for teens who learn to work the system. The most vivid image I'd ever experienced was when I was attending college and coaching a local Christian high school basketball team. The town I coached in was close to the border so we'd often travel down to the United States to play. Just before the first trip down, I was chatting with my younger brother who was now attending a different high school. We talked about the tournament and I showed him my team roster.

As he looked it over, he came across a name and said, "This student is an old friend of mine. You need to be really careful if you are going to take him across the border. He's apparently a known dealer in town."

We could not have been talking about the same kid. "He's a model student," I assured my brother. "This student works hard in school and he gets good grades. The teachers love him."

My brother said, "Yes, they do. But they love him for the wrong reasons. He says all the right things to the right people. He always comes to school with the perfect tie-knot, and he never breaks a school rule. This student is a decent basketball player, but at the school he goes to, he's learned to play their game the best."

I realize that deception can happen in any institution, regardless of whether the community has a strong vision or not, but deception runs rampant in communities where leaders place conformity before unity. Because really, anyone who conforms and sacrifices themselves in the process, essentially becomes a pretender. Those who do so unknowingly, eventually mature to a point where they resent the institution and all that it represents, which is tragic when the institution represents Christ. Those who are perceptive enough to manipulate the system, though they may possess an innate survival skill, potentially create a duplicitous façade, and walk an extremely precarious ridge. They mature into adulthood fully understanding they possess the ability to manipulate people in a way they can get whatever they want, and they also mature to a point of confusion. They know who they've been to get what they want, but they lack a clear understanding of their true selves. Thus, they eventually end up at a point in their journey where they feel completely disconnected from self, from others, from God. This may take years or decades, depending on the individual.

Until a few months ago, I never understood the potential damage institutional conformity can inflict on an individual. By God's divine hand, I met up with a student I hadn't talked to in years. We made it through the awkwardness of the initial conversation, caused by the fact that we both needed to be somewhere else. In the end, though his words spoke of all he'd accomplished, his eyes told a different story, one that deeply concerned me. They were devoid of the spark associated with a deep passion for life. At the end of the conversation, I told him I'd love to go for coffee with him so that we could relax and catch up, and he agreed to my request. I think he gave me his number thinking I'd never really call him.

I did, and a week later we sat in a coffee shop sipping lattes on a bleak winter evening. It did not take long for him to open up. This time, instead of talking of successes, he spoke of hurt. And Cameron did so in a way where he began with the outcome. He said, "A few weeks ago I tried to kill myself, but I'm doing better now. I'm medicated, and I spoke with a psychiatrist in the hospital about why maybe I'd try to do something like that to myself. I've tried before. This was not the first time. I think the first time I tried was in grade six, then again in grade 12. Really, I don't know the reason. It's not like I had a bad childhood or anything like that."

As we continued on in the conversation sometimes we delved deep trying to search for understanding. But really, there was no intention behind my search other than to rebuild a relationship with a student who I'd lost touch with for a few years. I simply listened in order to empathize with his hurt. So we spoke about the incident, we reminisced, we spoke of old acquaintances, and new friendships he'd formed since high school.

I never brought up faith. Although, at one point, he said, "No offense, Mr. Bird, but I'm no longer a Christian." Then he said, "I have done a lot of research and I can explain to you why evolution is fact. All science supports evolution." I replied, "I'm sure we could have a lengthy discussion as to our opposing views, but I'd rather not. Cameron, I'm not here to debate with you, and I'm not even here to try to reconvert you. I'm here to have coffee with a former student. I'm interested in your life, in you, that is all."

Then he inquired as to why I would not debate the topic with him. I replied, "We could talk about the issue, but I've discovered a truth beyond the debate. In the last year, I've spoken with hundreds of people, most of whom do not have Christ, and most of them have lived their lives to the fullest. They've made lots of money, traveled extensively, and built their dream houses. They've enjoyed life. And in doing so, they also carry a backpack full of experiences they have no idea what to do with. They carry around hurt, bitterness, and guilt. They've abused others, been abused themselves, been divorced, searched for meaning, struggled with identity, and chronically lived with insecurity. Most of them self-medicate, with food, with alcohol, or with drugs, some prescription and others illegal. Some have sons who've gone to jail, and others have children who've died. Some have children who live but who want nothing to do with them or vice versa. So we could debate right now about how this planet and its inhabitants came into existence, but really the more pressing issue is purpose. People search for purpose, and they want to know who they are. They want assurance that all the pain they've endured is worth something. And in order to uncover purpose, humans need a place to take all that burdens them. Faith offers me this. Christ offers humanity this."

We spoke of many subjects after the avoided debate, but Cameron kept revisiting my reasoning behind why I would not debate with him. The words made a deep connection with him. He did so until we were told by the barista it was closing time and then as we exited the coffee shop, Cameron said, "Mr. Bird, I have no idea who I am. I can be anything for anyone and that's what I've been my entire life. I can debate either side of a topic, or I can sit and listen and say nothing. I can be polite and respectful, and I can be rude and obnoxious. I can be the perfect gentleman in front of my girlfriend's parents, and be chauvinistic when I'm with my friends. I can sound intelligent in educated crowds and crass when I'm with the undereducated. I've been pretending so long I've lost myself."

I realize Cameron's life is complicated because everyone's life is complicated, but I can't help but wonder what part his Christian schooling played in his self-confusion. I'd never go so far as to blame the church or the school, but even if they were not a part of the problem, why were they not part of a solution? And will they be part of a solution before it's too late?

There's no conclusion to Cameron's story, which is good in a way. We continue to meet and discuss life, and build relationship. And each time we do, I'm reminded he is a poster child for Christian teens who've lost faith. He grew up in a Christian home. He attended church. He spent the entirety of his grade school years at a Christian institution, yet he has no idea who he is. He no longer believes purpose is found in Christ, or that it is the starting point of the journey to discovering self. Cameron grew up in the Christian community and now desires nothing to do with "the family of God." Why? Calvinists would say God simply did not choose Cameron, and Arminianists would say he may end up choosing God at any point in his journey. A conservative Christian would say Cameron was too exposed to the world too early, and a liberal Christian would say the Christian school sheltered him too much. A creationist would say Cameron is tainted by evolutionary ideology and does not know who he is because he believes he evolved; whereas, an evolutionary scientist would blame forced institutionalized beliefs for his lack of purpose.

What would Christ say? I suspect if this group approached him for a solution, he just might stoop down and write in the sand for a while and then when he straightened up he might respond, "There was a man who owned a vineyard ..." (Matthew 20). To which all those involved in the debate over Cameron's life might just figure Christ has no idea what he's talking about. What does grape growing have to do with the young man's salvation? I envision the debaters turning away to carry on their conversation, while Christ walks over and puts his arm around Cameron's shoulders and says, "May I join you on your journey? I have much to tell you about a man who has a vineyard, and I suspect you're in a place where you're ready to talk about vineyards." Then Jesus might carry on and tell Cameron about a landowner who hires the unemployed to work his fields. Those hired at the beginning of the day know exactly what they are going to earn for a wage: they will earn a standard day's wage for a day's work. But the landowner went out again and found workers standing around and asks them to come and work for him, yet he does not tell them what they will earn. He only informs them he will pay them whatever is right. He goes out again and finds more workers lacking work and makes them the same offer. Finally near the end of the day, he does the same with more unemployed laborers.

When it comes time to pay, the landowner pays those who worked only a fraction of the day a full day's wage. Those who trusted him to pay what is fair and right, he pays beyond what is fair and what is right. He does not pay them what they earned but exceeds that amount. Those who worked all day saw this and expected a larger wage, but when the owner comes to pay them, he gives them the same amount as those who started later on in the day. They grumble about this and the landowner responds by saying he has the right to do whatever he wants with his money. Then he says, "So the last will be first, and the first will be last" (Matthew 20:16 NIV). Your reward is not based on what you do; your reward is based on what I've done for you. I invite. You respond. And you become part of my vineyard. You're no longer in the marketplace waiting and wondering about the hopelessness of showing up every day searching for meaning, seeking purpose.

Those who show up early, our kids who have accepted Christ early on in life, face a greater challenge. When they compare their accomplishments rather than focus on God's generosity, they begin to apply their own reason and rationale to the way the master runs the vineyard, and this is a reason they can become disgruntled. The master, though, reminds each one who joined his workforce early that his generosity is only a portion of what he offers. Perhaps more importantly, he recruits individuals to his workforce so we no longer have to question our purpose, so that we no longer have to show up to the marketplace each morning wondering if we will make a connection. He provides us with purpose—tend to his vineyard. Our reward at the end of the day is heaven, and an individual can't receive more than an eternity in unadulterated, unrestrained relationship with God. Regardless of when they show up to the vineyard.

The other day I lived a metaphor reminding me of existence with Christ in the vineyard versus what we earn at the end of the day. Existence with him as we toil is much like a ferry ride I took. I traveled from one Pacific Island to a much smaller one, and when I embarked, I climbed the stairs on the boat as high as I could go. At the end of the staircase, I found an uncovered deck, like a viewing platform with bench seats. The sun shone unhindered by cloud but the north wind off the ocean made me wish I was wearing pants instead of shorts. A few other travelers found the upper deck as well, seated themselves for a minute or two and then must have decided against enduring the cool wind. As the ferry began moving, something strange happened. The wind stopped—well not really. All round me I could see the effects of the wind; the trees swayed and the waves kept cadence as the breeze directed them. Yet on the upper deck, I enjoyed the warmth of the sun without the north breeze. The direction of the boat and the speed of the boat matched the speed and direction of breeze, and allowed for me to enjoy a wind-free ride across the strait. I envision life to be like this, once we've been selected by the owner of the vineyard, and when we are not worried about what's fair and what's not fair—when we simply trust the master with all that happens in our lives. Regardless of wind or tempest, in the face of challenges and pain we trust God to bring us to a point where all is used for his glory. We simply trust God. We simply exist in his presence, not unfettered because as we toil and as we tend to the vineyard we see the storm's effects all around us, and not without pain and failure and hurt, but we trust the wine the master creates from our toil will be aged and perfect for all who come to drink the fruit of the vine. We endure the challenges because one day we will receive a reward for our day's work, not because we've earned what he gives us but because we've trusted God's words when he says he will pay what is fair and right.

Swinging with the Sweet Spot in Mind

No secret formula exists. I can't say with confidence that every student who moves from his or her home out to university or to the workforce, as long as he or she has grown up in an atmosphere of unity, and who understands God's will and purpose is surely going to follow Christ all of his or her days. With so many possibilities, with so many probabilities, with so many personalities, with so many internal forces, with so many external forces, all pulling our children this way and that, nothing we do can result in a guaranteed positive outcome. That said, what we do and the way we respond to them does have an enormous impact, which can be a force helping to steer them in a positive direction.

Years ago my wife and I took our kids to see *Toy Story 3*. Families packed into the theater, and the usual noise existed as with any other family movie in the theater. Infants cried because mom and dad brought little brother or sister even though they're too young to enjoy the movie. Mom and kid "slipping" past me in the middle of the movie because little Johnny drank a full two-liter worth of pop, and his bladder only holds half a liter. However, near the end of the movie, something different happened, something I'd never heard in a family movie experience before—parents crying. At the part where Andy has to leave and go off to college, the point where he has to give away his toys, I heard the noises associated with adult tears. I looked over at my wife to see her wipe the moisture from her eyes with the same napkin she used earlier to clean butter from our youngest son's fingers. At that, I felt a lump in my throat begin to form. I suppressed tears by reminding myself there was no way I was going to cry during a silly Pixar film.

When we drove away from the theatre my wife said, "What's the matter, honey?"

To which I emphatically responded, "Why would you say anything is the matter? I'm fine. There's nothing wrong."

About an hour later, after visiting my parents, and after taking the same route fifteen years earlier away from my parent's house when I began the nine hour drive from my hometown to university, my wife again said, "You okay, sweetie?" That's when it all came out. I could not suppress the throat lump any longer.

Tears flowed down my face as I blurted out, "Our boys are going to grow up, and they're going head off to university and nothing will ever be the same again. And it's all going to happen like that"—as I snapped my fingers together.

The film reminded me I am all too aware that the child-rearing years pass quickly. Every year during grade 12 parent/teacher interviews I see tears. Mostly moms, but some fathers start to cry when we begin to speak about what direction their child is planning to go the following year. My first year teaching the visible emotion caught me off guard, but now I stock up on Kleenex before the interviews. More often than not, through raw emotion, the parents coach me by letting me know how important it is to cherish your time with your children because it goes by way too quickly. One moment you're changing their diapers, and the next moment you're sitting with them at the table going over university calendars and selecting courses.

So what do we do in between? What do we do in order to give them the best opportunity to stay with Christ through it all? What do we do to ensure that they don't feel like they need to pretend or work the system? In this particular area, between self-discovery and faith discovery, between character authenticity and a connection to purpose, we walk a ridge with them. As their family we do all we can to become a community they can always trust and always comfortably return. This means sometimes we tell them the way it is, and sometimes we work through issues together. We seek forgiveness when we make a mistake so they learn they need to seek forgiveness when they make a mistake. We relate to our teens in a way that acknowledges their uniqueness, yet we constantly push them toward standards and goals. We teach them to take responsibility for their actions, and we give them freedom to make decisions for which they can take ownership. We allow them to engage in real life situations that benefit the greater community, rather than simply taking part in activities that gratify self. In other words, as a family we become a micro community of authenticity. And then we actively take part in a larger faith community where authenticity, unconditional love, grace, and forgiveness abound.

ENDNOTES

Chapter 1

1   Kingston, Anne. "Get Ready for Generation Z." *Maclean's Magazine.* July 21, 2014: 42–45. Print.

2   Ibid.

3   Ibid.

4   Dickey, Jack. "The Antisocial Network." *Time* magazine. July 7, 2014: 40–45. Print.

5   Ibid.

6   Ibid.

7   Zacchaeus Lyrics: youtube.com/watch?v=mV8wFANocHY&spfreload=1.

Chapter 3

8   "Essential 2013 Essential Facts about the Computer and Video Game Industry." *The Entertainment Software Association.* Web. May 12, 2014. <theesa.com>.

9   Van Der Meulen, Rob, and Janessa Rivera. "Gartner Says Worldwide Video Game Market to Total $93 Billion in 2013." *Gartner.* October 29, 2013. Web. August 14, 2014. <gartner.com/technology/home.jsp>.

10   "Statistics and Facts on Camping & Recreational Vehicles." *Statista: The Statistics Portal.* Web. November 24, 2014. <statista.com>.

11   "Statistics and Facts on Recreational Fishing." *Statista: The Statistics Portal.* Web. November 24, 2014. <statista.com>.

Chapter 6

12   Whitman, Walt. "O Captain! My Captain." *Poetry Foundation.* Web. November 1, 2014.

13   Ibid.

Chapter 7
[14] "The Writings of St. Francis of Assisi: The Canticle of the Sun." *Sacred Text Archive*. Web. October 1, 2014. <sacred texts.com/chr/wosf/wosf22.htm>.

Chapter 8
[15] Shakespeare, William. *Julius Caesar*: Act 5, scene 1. Web. August 18, 2014. <shakespeare-navigators.com/JC_Navigator/JC_5_1.html>.

Chapter 9
[16] Milton, John. "On His Blindness." *Cummings Study Guide*. January 1, 2008. Web. September 20, 2014.

[17] Ibid.

[18] Ibid.

Chapter 11
[19] *Indiana Jones and the Last Crusade*. *Wikiquote*. Web. October 20, 2014. <en.wikiquote.org/wiki/Indiana_Jones_and_the_Last_Crusade>.

[20] Ibid.

[21] Ibid.

Chapter 13
[22] Epstein, David. "Are Athletes Really Getting Faster, Better, Stronger?" *Ted*. March 1, 2014. Web. April 11, 2014. <ted.com>.

WORKS CITED

Dickey, Jack. "The Antisocial Network." *Time* magazine. July 7, 2014: 40–45. Print.

Donne, John. "Batter My Heart, Three Person'd God." *Poetry Foundation.* Web. June 16, 2014. <poetryfoundation.org/poem/173362>.

Epstein, David. "Are Athletes Really Getting Faster, Better, Stronger?" *Ted.* March 1, 2014. Web. April 11, 2014. <ted.com>.

"Essential 2013 Essential Facts about the Computer and Video Game Industry." *The Entertainment Software Association.* Web. May 12, 2014. <theesa.com>.

Holy Bible: English Standard Version. Crossway Bibles, 2001. BibleGateway.com. Web. November 21, 2014.

Holy Bible: King James Version. BibleGateway.com. Web. November 24, 2014.

Holy Bible: New International Version. Colorado Springs: Biblica, 2011. BibleGateway.com. Web. November 21, 2014.

Holy Bible: New Living Translation. Illinois: Tyndale House Foundation, 2013. BibleGateway.com. Web. November 24, 2014.

Hopkins, Lyn. "Zacchaeus for Kids with Lyrics." YouTube. Web. October 5, 2014.

Indiana Jones and the Last Crusade. *Wikiquote*. Web. October 20, 2014. <en.wikiquote.org/wiki/ Indiana_Jones_and_the_Last_Crusade>.

Kingston, Anne. "Get Ready for Generation Z." *Maclean's Magazine*. July 21, 2014: 42–45. Print.

Milton, John. "On His Blindness." *Cummings Study Guide*. January 1, 2008. Web. September 20, 2014.

Peterson, Eugene H. *The Message* (2002). BibleGateway.com. Web. November 21, 2014.

Shakespeare, William. *Julius Caesar*: Act 5, scene 1. Web. August 18, 2014. <shakespeare-navigators.com/JC_Navigator/JC_5_1. html>.

Shakespeare, William. *Macbeth*: Act 5, scene 5. Web. June 11, 2014. *<shakespeare-navigators.com/macbeth/T55.html>*.

"Statistics and Facts on Camping & Recreational Vehicles." *Statista: The Statistics Portal*. Web. November 24, 2014. <statista. com>.

"Statistics and Facts on Recreational Fishing." *Statista: The Statistics Portal*. Web. November 24, 2014. <statista.com>.

Van Der Meulen, Rob, and Janessa Rivera. "Gartner Says Worldwide Video Game Market to Total $93 Billion in 2013." *Gartner*. October 29, 2013. Web. August 14, 2014. <gartner.com/ technology/home.jsp>.

Whitman, Walt. "O Captain! My Captain." *Poetry Foundation.* Web. November 1, 2014.

"The Writings of St. Francis of Assisi: The Canticle of the Sun." *Sacred Text Archive.* Web. October 1, 2014. <sacred-texts.com/chr/wosf/wosf22.htm>.